John L. Casey

Ethics in the Financial Marketplace

SCUDDER

Published by: Scudder, Stevens & Clark
                 345 Park Avenue
                 New York, NY 10154
                 (212) 326-6200

Coordination: Davia B. Temin
                 Eileen Winrock

Editorial: Elisabetta di Cagno
                 Laury A. Kassell
                 Olga M. Hadji

Design: De Plano Design, Inc., New York

Library of Congress Catalog Card Number: 88-90753

ISBN: 0-9620632-0-7

Printed in the United States of America

*I dedicate this effort to the
many who demonstrate ethics
in the financial marketplace,
including:*

*Seven leaders of the
Investment Counsel
Association of America in the
1960s who brought general
ethical concepts to bear on
specific factual conflicts of
interest in a changing marketplace:
David Babson
H. Williamson Ghriskey
George S. Johnston
James H. Lawrence
Dwight Rogers
Charles W. Shaeffer
Henry B. Thielbar*

*A farsighted government official:
John S. R. Shad*

*A wise security analyst/philosopher:
Irving Kahn*

*A charismatic teacher:
Stanley Hauerwas*

*The codirectors of the
Institute on Ethics in
Management and the Center
for Responsible Management:
Charles W. Powers
Barbara Ley Toffler.*

Introduction

For over twenty-five years Jack and I have worked together at Scudder, Stevens & Clark and with the Investment Counsel Association of America (I.C.A.A.). Both organizations have been built on the ethical concept of unbiased investment advice to clients, seeking to identify in advance—and then eliminate—situations where our self-interest conflicts with our clients' interests.

Jack's book helps each of us draw and redraw a personal blueprint to guide us in making ethical judgments in complex transactions. There is no similar "how to" work that meets that important need at the entry level in business generally and the financial industry in particular. Of equal importance, using basic English rather than ethics jargon, it refreshes those of us who have been in the financial industry for our professional lives.

The book describes a group of fictional saints and sinners from the world of finance: traders, directors, shareholders, pension managers, planners, and supervisors. They are faced with problems of sentiment, insider information, and conflicts of interest.

Using shortcuts and models, we are invited to improve the quality, depth, and farsightedness of our management decisions by bringing personal insights to bear on analysis, planning, and implementation. We are introduced to paired concepts such as paternalism and participation, coercion and control, which help us to include our personal values in our decision making despite limited time. Because the cases are more than vignettes and contain the ambiguities and dilemmas of "real life," no single right solution is proposed.

In practice, I.C.A.A. members have historically received no investment banking, brokerage transaction, or dealer fees. Our personal security transaction codes are designed to put the client first. Thus, allocations of clients' brokerage by many investment advisers are based on best execution without reference even to new business referrals; we do not make loans to portfolio companies. Rather than resolving each conflict of interest fairly, we have opted for seeking to eliminate the conflicts of interest.

As Jack points out, ethical management, involving as it does a special sensitivity to those who are affected by our decisions, is sophisticated management in the best sense of the word.

I can think of no one better suited than Jack Casey to be the author of this book. During his many years of activity in the investment advisory field, not only has he demonstrated leadership and vision but has always approached operating and business questions with a concept of putting first the interests of the client and the investor. Often he has demonstrated this just by asking the question, "Is it good for the client?" He has shown the way to the answer which resolves conflicts on the highest ethical basis.

We are happy to publish this first edition.

> George S. Johnston
> Chairman and CEO
> Scudder, Stevens & Clark, Inc.

Contents

About the Author

Jack Casey began work on *Ethics in the Financial Marketplace* at the suggestion of the Financial Analysts Research Foundation, receiving the 1984 Leubsdorf Award for the manuscript. His object was to provide a readable "how-to book" on ethics where none seemed to exist, specifically adding an ethical dimension to the responsibilities of professionals in the financial industry.

His interests have been eclectic. After Harvard Law School he worked with Simpson Thacher & Bartlett, one of the largest Wall Street law firms, and has spent the last twenty-five years with Scudder, Stevens & Clark, one of the country's largest investment managers. He is a managing director of Scudder and his primary current responsibilities are in connection with financial services to members of the American Association of Retired Persons.

He has served as a director of Scudder Development Fund, Scudder Capital Growth Fund and Scudder International Fund, director, president, and chairman of the Investment Counsel Association of America, chairman of the Annual Investment Management and Mutual Funds Conference, a member of the U.S. Secretary of Labor's Advisory Council on Employee Welfare and Pension Benefit Plans, chairman of the Investment Committee and a member of the Committee of Lawyers' Role in the Search for Peace of the Association of the Bar of the City of New York, a director of Cavitron Corporation, president of the Louis Braille Foundation for Blind Musicians, commander of the Willard Straight Post of the American Legion, and national chairman of Youth for Eisenhower.

His current public responsibilities include the Advisory Board of the Council for International Understanding of the Myrin Institute, convener of the '40 Acts Committee, board membership of Bennett College Foundation, the Institute on Ethics in Management, the Harvard Club of New York City (of which he is treasurer), St. David's School (of which he is Board president), and the Center for the Study of World Religions of Harvard University.

In his spare time he is a paterfamilias, plays clarinet, windsurfs, and jogs.

This is a "how-to" book for financial managers about adding ethical perspectives to complex daily situations and making sounder decisions. It provides a structure through which managers may more wisely apply their own knowledge, insights, and perspectives to the situation at hand. It is not a "code of aphorisms."

In 1979 I participated in the second Institute on Ethics in the Management of Public and Private Institutions, meeting Charles W. Powers and Barbara Ley Toffler, the codirectors of the Institute, and Stanley Hauerwas, the director of my working group. Their goal and the achievement of the Institute was to identify the readings and communications system that would teach business managers how to include ethical considerations in decisions.

Their breakthrough was to identify issue categories that are manager-friendly, use the speech of daily life, and, sensitizing us, invite ethical judgments. These categories are:

- Coercion. The manager should not be deprived of control over the decision by external pressures ranging from peer attitudes to threats, or impose such similar pressures on people affected by the decisions of the manager.
- Competing claims. Conflicts of interest, including the self-interest of the decision maker, must be accurately identified in order to be properly resolved.
- Physical environment. "Spaceship Earth" and "future generations" are parties to our decisions.
- Paternalism. This is not universally desirable: a manager's "do good" decision may seem to be in the best interest of the "beneficiary," but the very lack of participation by the beneficiary may distort the result and undo the good.
- Personal integrity. Personal values are an essential part of managers' ethical conduct; their business lives must be consistent with those values.

Subsequently the Financial Analysts Research Foundation, through John Gillis, their counsel, and Richard de Mong, the executive director, invited me to write a book applying ethical concepts to the financial industry. It took a year of thrashing around for me to find a way of getting a handle on the subject.

I had just finished an unpublished novel, *Seward's Folly,* that played with some ethical and moral dilemmas. Professor David J. Frietzsche of the University of Nevada-Reno suggested that I use a technique, which he has since used, of factual vignettes with analysis.* Barbara Toffler's galley proof of *Tough Choices/Managers Talk Ethics* (1986, John Wiley & Sons, Inc. New York), gave me a key idea: At the heart of her book are the edited texts of interviews she conducted with twenty or more managers. That encouraged me to move from vignettes to more lengthy case studies, which would involve fictional managers, but the real ambiguities, time pressures, and need for close calls in financial managers' lives. (Unless there is a specific reference to a real situation, the interviews, references, monologues, and dialogues should be read as symbols, not as reports of actual incidents.)

To add structure to the discussion section I accepted three classical perspectives on ethics:

> Utilitarian, evaluating behavior in terms of its social conse-
> quences; rights, emphasizing the entitlements of individuals;
> and justice, focusing on the distributional effects of actions or
> policies[XV-1].

The chapters unfolded slowly with a lot of help from the secretarial and word processing staff at Scudder and some from my Apple II computer. Jamie Shillinglaw, who had recently graduated from Columbia, read, researched, and redirected. Irving Kahn of the Foundation read, commented, and encouraged me to direct the message to persons with different levels of experience and sophistication. The manuscript received the 1984 Karl Leubsdorf Memorial Fund Award and the Financial Analysts Federation and Institute of Chartered Financial Analysts found the manuscript useful for their *Standards of Practice Handbook.* However, the Analysts Foundation decided it would not publish the book and I set aside the project.

Two years later with the antiethic of greed in the headlines and the courts, I thought with irony that 1987 was the fiftieth year of the Investment Counsel Association of America, which had been organized to promote a special ethical principle of "client first." The members, including my firm Scudder, Stevens & Clark, have long adhered to self-imposed rules on personal security transactions; the client interest does come first, prohibiting investment counsel from making commercial loans to companies in which the clients invest and receiving compensation tied to the number or value of transactions entered into by the client. This is not pie in the sky: it has worked for fifty years for I.C.A.A. members and its standards have been used as a model by many regulators. Several of its standards of practice have even been adopted by nonmembers and by regulatory agencies. So I am a believer that there are ethics in the financial marketplace. Thinking of the involvement Scudder and I have with the Association, it seemed that a book on ethics would be a fine way to celebrate the I.C.A.A.'s past and present.

At that point publication of the book became a project broadly supported by my friends and colleagues at Scudder. Michael Griffin encouraged me to get the book out to the marketplace where its ideas could begin to work. George Johnston, (whose matrix in the 1960s for qualification of firms for I.C.A.A. membership is still alive and well) endorsed the idea. My friend Laury Kassell chipped in as wordsmith and idea sculptor. Davia Temin developed a program for publication and persuaded three of her friends to help. Elisabetta di Cagno agreed to act as editor, which was a ten-strike as Elisabetta's ear and eye are tuned to Strunk & White's *The Elements of Style;* her "rewrite" suggestions have been exciting to respond to and the book has acquired new integrity under her kind tutelage; Marco de Plano and Nicolae Zeletineanu produced a series of excellent cover designs reflecting the dynamic point of view of the book and its financial focus.

Many others have provided essential help as models, advisers, supporters, and transcribers. That resulted in a multigenerational participation in this book of fictional interviews dealing with very real topics such as trading desks, fiduciary investment management, proxy voting, insider information, and mergers and acquisitions. Consistent with the concept of the Institute on Ethics in Management, the effort is to be specific rather than ethereal, using common words rather than ethics jargon, providing tools to help managers consciously apply personal value systems to daily problems.

---

*David J. Frietzche and Helmut Becker, *Academy of Management Journal,* "Linking Management Behavior to Ethical Philosophy—An Empirical Investigation," 1984 Vol. 27 No. 1 pp. 166–175.

Chapter 1

What are Ethics, Anyway?
Managers and Complex Problems

Is being ethical a matter of "dealer's choice?" Ethics are so often
discussed in words that are unfamiliar, ethereal, stuffy, technical,
or inappropriate for our role and self-image that managers hear the
words and say "not for me," "too abstract," and "not quantifiable."
"Ethics" itself can be a put-off word, and the following comments
can easily be heard in the modern business world:

Our firm is very ethical. I check things out with our legal
department whenever things are doubtful.

Ethics is an adult version of the Boy Scout Oath. It has very
little to do with real decisions.

I think of ethics in management as meaning that you do a good
practical job. The point is to be professional, to focus on probabilities and fairness.

When people talk of ethics they lose their professionalism as
managers. Ethics is just not quantifiable. It's almost an excuse
from being held accountable.

Being an ethical manager isn't something you can look up in
the dictionary. It depends on the facts. Sometimes the best thing
for shareholders in a takeover threat may be to stay independent
rather than take a couple of extra bucks this year and have the
company broken up. Also, don't forget the employees who work
for the company and would be out of a job; they are part of the
company, too.

Ethics is your gut feeling; it's hitting your level of comfort.

There are different kinds of ethics for different kinds of people.
People have different jobs. It's who you work for and what they
are expecting of you. Let's say you are the controller of the

target company in a tender offer. Aren't you going to act in the opposite way from the controller of the raider company?

A book on ethics in the financial industry? Sounds like a very short book!

However incomplete or facetious these comments may appear, each has a germ of truth that we need to recognize in order to understand ethics in the financial marketplace.

Both ethical concepts and ethical jargon put managers off. Words like "contextual," "normative," and "paradigm" can quickly discourage an audience of practical people. A simpler vocabulary is important. In many disciplines that is not possible, but in ethics we can go a long way with common words. The concepts then become workable. In fact, every day we apply ethics unconsciously, and so our everyday vocabulary can do the job of defining and explaining ethics.

Being pragmatic is okay. Managers justifiably consider themselves to be practical. Accordingly, it is logical to begin our exploration of ethics from a perspective of pragmatism: does the decision work in light of the effects it will have on people and the available alternatives? For example, taking into account cost and financial reward, is it "practical" in the long run to leave a strip mining site behind, disheveled and dangerous after its exploitation? Pragmatism encompasses not just the present but also the future: future risks of harm, future costs, and future decisions. Yet, if the manager concludes that leaving that mining site unrestored makes sense, the analysis is not over. A further question must be asked: is leaving mining sites unrestored generally undesirable?[1-1] What kinds of results can one expect if that decision sets a precedent and becomes the general rule?

The best specific decision and the best overall rule can conflict. We know this from our daily observations. The courses of action implicit in the role we play may differ substantially from the courses of action our analysis suggests. We have to choose. A legislator who voted for a fifty-five mile-an-hour speed limit for automobiles has no hesitation in driving sixty-five miles an hour to get a child to a doctor. Each course of action may be designed to achieve a social good. The legislative rule deals with the precedent: there is a risk of social harm from widespread decentralization of a decision on how fast cars may travel. The risk of harming the child by delaying medical treatment is seen to outweigh the benefits of the rule, even though the violation may have unpleasant legal consequences such as the loss of a driving license.

Managers continuously judge the probable effects of their actions on customer satisfaction, stock prices, employee morale, and corporate growth. Thus, it is not difficult for such professionals as a class to push further, adding a dimension of ethical concern to their analyses by systemizing the probable effects of a corporate decision. Obvious benefits will be identified for some individuals and groups and clear disadvantages will be identified for others. Moreover, security analysts who are both spectators and participants in the world of business have a significant ethical role to play. Trained as they are to examine and resolve close questions, they can also process decisions on what may be harmful and what the net good appears to be rather than just report the actions of others.

Being fair—my rights versus your rights. In the world of the manager, fairness and an individual's rights are dealt with spontaneously and unconsciously. As transactions become more complex, the unconscious becomes insufficient and it is necessary to deliberately sort justice, trade-offs, private conscience, and "gut feelings." Being just and respecting human rights are not identical. They have subtly different starting points and results. Justice begins with the decision maker who says, "*I* will treat others fairly." The perspective of rights proceeds from the point of view of others, those who, affected by your decision, say "respect my rights." Each vantage point has its strengths and its own Achilles' heel. The mantle of justice can lead to autocratic and paternalistic behavior. A litany of rights can lead to weak leadership based on Gallup polls. There are also schizophrenic aspects. Pragmatism, rights, and justice are good tools, but each can justify a different conclusion; moreover we can easily (and unconsciously) choose a system that supports a narrow self-interest and be unaware that ethical analysis has been misused.

It is interesting to observe how freely some Congressional candidates speak out for the rights of their constituents when they are campaigning for election and then change their position in Congress, where their job is to balance competing interests. On the other hand, the most responsible politicians anticipate both at campaign time and while in office when too much attention to the rights of one particular constituency puts an unacceptable burden on another with different interests, risks, dimensions, and rights. The same need holds true for business managers who wish to add an ethical dimension to these decisions when choosing between being pragmatic, fair, or respectful of the rights of others. The consequent different results should be anticipated.

Certainly we should avoid selecting a single theory on the ground that it supports our self-interest: that is rhetoric, not ethics. But we can go further. If we separately employ each of these perspectives—being pragmatic, being just, and being protective of an individual's rights—we avoid being trapped by rhetoric into an unprocessed instinctive choice of our short-term self-interest or into an accidental choice! In combination, the insight afforded by the three clarify and focus what could be a one-sided factual situation, providing a three-dimensional analysis of the consequences of decision making.

Consider the ethical interplay as corporate managements have gained and exercised greater control over the governing machinery of corporations. This trend has developed its own momentum, causing the checks and balances available from shareholders, even sophisticated institutional shareholders, to atrophy. Many of the current headline issues occur in this context. Fifty years ago, management/ shareholder relations were based on several accepted premises:

- The management knew more about the business than shareholders did, and therefore management's judgment on all matters of policy was to be accepted.
- The management had no responsibility for the prices at which the company's securities sell.
- Shareholders who disapproved of any major policy of the management could sell their stock in the company.[1-2]

Whether or not these statements were true at the time, many public shareholders were individuals with limited interest, training, and information. Today, when public stockholders are well-informed regarding their investments, these statements are clearly untrue. The current constellation of U.S. shareholders is dominated by institutions with access to the most experienced and sophisticated advice concerning their investments. Today's reality is:

- External analysts know as much about a business as management and are paid by investors to second-guess managerial judgment.
- Through options and tenure, management has a personal interest in the price at which a company's securities are sold and in increasing the public interest and knowledge of the company.
- Shareholders who disapprove of corporate policy have more than one option, but may have to fight for their position.

Let's assume corporate management proposes to impair the vote of its public shareholders. What can the public shareholders and their investment advisers do in response? There are four choices: they can remain silent; they can notify management of any disagreement in advance of action; they can alert management after the decision has been taken; or they can sell the security.[1-3] The combination of the first and last choices has for fifty years been the "Wall Street Rule." Rule or no rule, if the security is priced on a relatively attractive basis it is unlikely that the stock will actually be sold despite the policy disagreement. So under the "Rule," the reality turns out to be an endorsement of management by default. Moreover, silence on the part of the institutional investor during the policy considerations may have tipped the balance in favor of the undesired change. A dialogue between the investment adviser and corporate management, or even some form of one-way communication, makes more sense.

The financial business is filled with conflicting interests. Investment counselors and corporate management alike find themselves with more than one constituency and a daily need to respond to each. Proposed mergers and acquisitions can make objective analysis especially difficult. In deciding whether to fight or cooperate in the takeover, managements experience severe pulls with respect to job preservation—their own jobs. That conflict never can be eliminated, but there are ways in which it can be handled. The independent directors of the corporation are free to evaluate alternatives objectively.[1-4] While nonmanagement directors may not have shown significant independence from the objectives of management, they have the potential to add important value, tailor-making a decision to the needs of the various groups affected and the negotiation opportunities that are available.

By way of contrast a proposal suggested by Esterbrook and Fishel in the Harvard Law Review would prohibit self-help by target company boards against takeovers.[1-5] The authors suggest that management be required to remain passive in the face of such an assault:

> Thus, management should not propose antitakeover charter or bylaw amendments, file suits against the offeror, acquire a competitor of the offeror in order to create an antitrust obstacle to the tender offer, buy or sell shares in order to make the offer more costly, give away to some potential "white knight" valuable corporate information which might call for a competing bid, or initiate any other defensive tact to defeat a tender offer.

While the frustration resulting from selfish responses by management may make such prohibitions appealing, that is no long-term answer. Blanket solutions ignore the added value of human beings who analyze the facts in a specific situation and act in good faith. The Esterbrook and Fishel proposal assumes that *Ethics in the Financial Marketplace* is a book with blank pages, a self-contradictory phrase—an oxymoron—like "jumbo shrimp," "diamond ring," "civil war," and "ill health," only less funny.

There is evidence that the pursuit of excellence and greater ethical input from corporate and financial managers has been on the upswing.[1-6] Coincidentally, however, the antiethic of greed has reached headline proportions, inviting the knee-jerk response of "ethical" groups to outlaw overreaching by managements, to pass a law. Yet laws can undercut ethics. They can bypass the exercise by responsible managers of discretion. Moreover, by drawing a line they imply that permissible conduct is ethical conduct. The long-term answer to future ethical questions must rather rest in the hands of informed professionals who are part of the industry on a day-to-day basis; professionals who have the analytical tools of bread-and-butter marketplace issues, a keen sense of the values involved, and a willingness to resolve ethical dilemmas. The problem is that few managers (financial or corporate) have any systematic ability to process the ethical dimension.

We need to find people who have the education and skills necessary to assess and integrate the varied financial, political, and social content of today's business problems and who are particularly suited to assume ethical responsibilities. As a class, financial analysts, trust officers, and investment counsel have such characteristics. In a sense ethics is just another set of principles that they can apply to a complex set of facts.

Chapter 2

Zen and the Art of Ethical Analysis
The Facts and the Role

When the Wall Street trumpets blare takeover, tender offer, and crisis, investment managers and analysts are put under severe time pressures that can short-circuit their regular procedures. In such circumstances identifying our specific self-interest at the outset becomes important so it will not dominate our conclusion. Managing the pension fund of the target or the raider can distort judgment with respect to unrelated parties who are also clients of the management firm. Having a partner on the board of a competitor that would be adversely affected by the merger can get in the way.

Early in the game, when analyzing the deal, it makes sense to list the people and groups—management, shareholders, employees, competitors, suppliers—who will be affected by the situation, and identify the probable benefits and burdens that will flow to these groups from different decisions. As the action develops so will your evaluation. You can be helped by a three-branch decision tree. One branch, the pragmatic branch, directs us to the decision that, in our judgment, best balances the competing interests. Concepts of justice and rights form the other branches of the decision tree. After all, it is the shareholders' money that will be used to defend the corporation against the takeover, yet an aggressive defense may benefit an entrenched and fearful management to the disadvantage of the shareholders.

This should not be the end of the analysis. Even if management's decision favors self-protection, if the shareholders are benefitted by such a defense the motive of the management is less significant. We must ask what is happening in this situation. What are the potential dangers, and who is in danger? Whose claims come first among the competing groups? As a fiduciary you need to underscore any group that is depending on fiduciary judgment. Such a claim on your judgment can override any other. If some group may suffer death and dismemberment, can that risk be justified under any circumstances? Questions of ethics cannot be handled by a computer screen. In fact, nothing can be further from the fact, as ethical dimension decisions are the only training for further ethical decisions.

Professional analysts are in a good position, both intellectually and situationally, to combine basic ethical principles with complex and changing facts. By virtue of their fiduciary experience they also can handle the hardest (and easiest) task—identifying self-interest. We always have a personal interest of some sort and can be in charge only if we know what that interest is, discounting and subordinating it in favor of an open-book examination and an unbiased decision. It is a rare utilitarian who will not agree that justifying pragmatism in seeking social good does not mean "me first!"

Consider this scenario: our first fictionalized company, Middleton Genetics Inc., feels threatened by a proposal of an outsider to buy it for cash. Management proposes to its board five-year employment contracts between the company and each of the seven top executives, doubling each individual's current benefits if and when there is an unfriendly merger and the executive leaves. The president argues that (a) such an account payable will slow down any unfriendly takeover; (b) the board will be able to act at its own pace in the best interests of Genetics; (c) no financial burden is being placed on Genetics as the payment will not be triggered until (and unless) there is a merger; (d) costs will be borne by the acquiring company, not the current shareholders; (e) the executives will receive the support they need to do a good job in managing the company. This type of employment contract, sometimes referred to as "a golden parachute" or "golden handcuffs" can be a very effective tool in discouraging tender offers—and in launching the managers in question on a golden yacht should the merger occur.

Are the president's statements true? The private interest of the executives is clearly at the heart of the proposal, and the board is put in a position where its personal ties to management make it easy to bless the proposal. That is not to imply that the merger should be accepted, merely that it is always a good idea to apply a discount factor to points made with a large self-interest content, and also, for the board to respond with its own analysis. The board needs to test whether it is in the interest of Genetics (employees, management, and shareholders) to slow down or frighten away a takeover. What is the likely price per share? What is the price of the employment agreements? Nothing is free: if the acquiring company must pay the executives, some of that money will almost certainly be diverted from the target shareholders.

This process can bring the board back to the tests it regularly employs when approving compensation packages: reviewing competitive salary rates (including termination benefits), the contributions made by each individual to the company, and the current ability of the corporation to make such a commitment. When approaching the decision in this systematic manner, it is not necessary for the board to conclude that management is overreaching or greedy in order to reach a contrary conclusion: the disagreement need not be *ad hominem*.

With the structure for systematic decision making in place, the board can consider alternatives to an unfriendly takeover that can hurt the shareholders. "Golden parachutes" are harshly criticized by the media and Congress: such arrangements are seen as lead balloons that sink the shareholders' prospects for an advantageous sale of shares. Whether these accusations are true or false, it is clear that corporate managements have generated poor publicity for such proposals. Thus, it is not surprising that in 1984 Congress barred corporations from deducting from taxable income any "excess parachute payment" compensation.[II-1]

The negative media and legislative responses may have arisen because businesses did not properly explain their actions, or because managers did in fact act irresponsibly in allotting special compensation to themselves. Either way, in this situation there is a lesson for a good manager thinking toward the future: some people consider it akin to embezzlement when managers decide to reward themselves dramatically at the shareholders' expense.

Keep in mind that for Congress to prohibit tax deduction of compensation three times the employee's base, contingent on a change in corporate control, does not mean that a deduction of two times base is proper. Directors always have an obligation that they are paid to exercise: fair judgment on behalf of the shareholders. Even if a management payment is not an "excess parachute payment" it may not be in the interest of the corporation.

There was a moment in the 1980s when the opportunity for reducing specific government regulation of business had political momentum and some philosophical basis. Many people believed that good-faith decisions independently arrived at by citizens provided greater social good than actions compelled by a central agency. It was thought that the wisest use of a government agency's power was to establish guidelines and objectives, allowing citizens to decide how to achieve these goals rather than allowing government to institute 100 detailed "how-to" regulations. With the scandals resulting from the theft of insider information by Ivan Boesky, Dennis Levine, and others that moment may have passed.

If so, business itself is to blame. The businessperson who over-reaches is a pariah damaging the regulatory environment for the regulators, the regulated, and the beneficiaries. When opportunities for self-regulation are handled selfishly and notoriously some other way of protecting the public interest is developed, often a legislative common denominator. However, the legislative process has not been concluded. A manager looking at a broad framework can justify self-restraint solely on the grounds of long-term self-interest for business in general. This view reinforces the ethical imperative to act fairly.

Management compensation agreements in the face of a proposed acquisition may or may not be improper. Term contracts can help a corporation attract and retain top people or they can result in pork barrel deals. The key difference lies in the facts upon which the management decision concerning the agreements is based. In 1980 in real life such an issue was presented to the board of Cavitron Corporation. The independent directors, led by the chairman, William G. Weld, initiated a proposal for term contracts for a few senior executives of a corporation that was facing a possible takeover by an unfriendly party.

Cavitron had sales of around $40 million and stock listed on the American Exchange. It had a number of excellent specialized products, including a state-of-the-art method for doctor's office removal of cataracts, an industry-standard product for the ultrasonic cleaning of teeth, and a laser surgery device with potential for breakthrough cancer surgery. Several years of high interest rates and inflation, slow payment by customers, and difficulties of inventory control had depressed the stock price to under $10 a share despite a coincident expansion of sales. Cavitron had come through difficulties with very attractive earning estimates and the stock moved up in price.

Then came a suitor, Cooper Laboratories, a public company, aggressively managed, with a history of forced acquisitions and some complementary products. The Cavitron board was not anxious to sell out or merge, but recognized the likelihood that there would be long drawn-out negotiations with the suitor to test the proposal and the alternatives. It also concluded that it was likely that Cavitron management would be deemed redundant if Cooper's overture was successful. This meant the executives' justifiable concern about their careers and compensation could seriously influence their ability to manage regular business, let alone negotiate the best deal for shareholders. Up to that point key executives had not yet written employment contracts. The contracts initiated by the independent directors were not contingent but immediate, the level of compensation was set at the level currently being paid, and the term was for three years.

The executives remained with the company during the stressful period of hot and cold negotiations, ultimately negotiating a cash deal with Cooper Laboratories at a price that was three times the trading price at the beginning of the exercise. The deal worked out very well for the shareholders. On the other hand, the key Cavitron executives did lose their jobs with the company. The contracts were not overly generous but they did provide a timely psychological bonus for the executives during the negotiations, a bridge period after the deal was struck with Cooper Laboratories, and a result that was helpful to both the shareholders and executives.

The starting point for the Cavitron board was not how to block a known deal but how to help those who were on the spot to act in the shareholders' interest, building up or refusing the offer as the facts required. The board looked at the needs of the corporation, trying to balance the interests of the shareholders and the employees in a concerned way. In other words, the strategy was not a legalistic formula to drive away the suitor, but was based on respect for the persons involved. The contract certainly did not cause the executives to act responsibly in their negotiations; there would have been all sorts of subtle ways of putting their own interests first. The board was counting on their loyalty and good faith; the package was a small step affirming the board's real respect for the management in the face of an unexpected and tense situation. In turn, the contractual handshake provided a way for the executives to look beyond the crisis of the moment and act as fiduciaries. It did not skew the conclusion but was consistent with the company's either staying independent or merging, as the situation evolved. The success of this strategy was foreshadowed in a universal rule created by Harvard Law School Professor W. Barton Leach:[II-2] average people who are on the spot can solve a future problem much better than can the brightest planner in advance. As Professor Leach wrote in 1940, "To regulate events in 1960 the judgment of a mediocre mind on the spot is incomparably preferable to the guess in 1940 of the greatest man who ever lived."

Whether the reason is sophisticated self-interest or loyalty to a broad constituency, managers who exercise due regard for the interests of others increase the likelihood that regulators will treat them as managers who will act responsibly in the future. The reverse is also true: managers who act as though deregulation has erased public policy have missed the point and will press government to reenter the arena of private business. The concerned manager who is on the spot and knows the facts can also do better than government in terms of ethics, balancing specific conflicting interests to achieve specific social good. Where there is a will there is a way.

Chapter 3

"Trust Me"
Fiduciaries and the Bottom Line

The line of separation between self-interest and client-interest is clear in the instance of the professional trustee acting as a fiduciary for beneficiaries before all other interests, including his or her own. From that client-first perspective, the trustee is given the job of adjusting investment risk policy, income goal, and capital invasions in light of conflicting interests of different generations, different tax brackets, and the differing needs of the separate beneficiaries. The trustee seeking to be a combination of Solomon, Justice Cardozo, and Bernard Baruch is doomed to fall short. But good faith and corporate disinterestedness are achievable.

Consider the first of our fictionalized heroes, Rusty Merrick, who upon graduating from business school joined the corporate loan department of a medium-sized bank and trust company we will call Midwest. He brings investment banking insights that had not previously been available in the company to the loan department, and helps to restructure and save two important customer relationships for the bank. In light of the outstanding success of this effort, he is identified as a potential member of senior management and given an early promotion to vice president with a roving assignment to troubled areas. At his suggestion the long-term planning committee is established, which would report directly to the bank's president. Merrick becomes secretary of the committee. After its first meeting, Merrick is asked to focus on the major concern of the bank's chief operating officer: the lagging revenues and increasing expenses of the trust department. For several years the trust department fees from both trust and custody relationships have, at best, been in line with expenses. Salaries are not competitive with those of independent investment managers and good investment personnel have been lost; poor portfolio performance has proved inhibiting in attracting new business. Profits are marginal or nonexistent.

As he looks at the trust department Merrick defines his job in terms of the bank as a whole:

> Calling a spade a spade, the job of the trust department is to help attract and retain upscale banking customers. Its products and services have to be tested by how profitable they are. Actions must be justified by the bottom line. Otherwise, we might as well sell it off.
>
> I'm not exactly in the trust department, but more a liaison between top management and the people over here. I bring a fresh look to the picture. That's why I'm here, getting these folks up to speed.
>
> A lot of the trust types are still living back in the 1970s, when performance was ignored and service was everything. Times have changed. They're nice enough people, well-educated and all that, but they are gun-shy and it is costly for the bank. There is more performance awareness by customers now, but our investment performance stays dull, dull, dull.
>
> What a mismatch: a big staff and a lot of small trusts, each of which is administered separately! A rich guy dies, taxes are paid, and the rest gets split up into half a dozen separate trusts. The smaller the account, the more painful our fixed costs.
>
> My goal is to consolidate, to get the assets of the individual trusts into our new common trust fund. That way we get a single person making the investment decision and, hopefully, we can build up enough transaction volume to get the brokers' attention, too—get their ideas on the hot stocks for the trust department and get their loan business for the bank.
>
> We've got to have an investment record that we can advertise. Get two or three birds with that one stone: we can then make a profit on the small trusts we have and attract some big accounts. What I've been doing in the personal trust area is a prelude. The money is not in the personal area these days. The really big fees are in pension trusts.
>
> Success in marketing doesn't mean that we'll have profits; we'll also have to change our system. As we get more accounts we'll actually have to add new software and more specialized marketing, client relations people—especially in the pension area— and a lot of high-fee client service. There will be some change in the personnel, too, and that's part of why the old crocks are dragging their feet, hanging on to the old way of doing things.

Why not?

We all know high-energy, efficient executives like Merrick and can appreciate the pressures he places on the trust officers. His loyalty to the bank (career), loyalty to the customer (performance), and loyalty to the almighty bottom line (profits) will be very hard for the trust staff to resist. Yet the trust personnel have been correctly trained to put the needs and expectations of the customer first, and that concept is given short shrift by Merrick. Career progress versus obsolescence is the choice he poses.

Merrick sees the trust department people as slowing his plan to systemize and make more efficient the administration of trust accounts, particularly smaller accounts. That may be a correct view but it is incomplete. The "old crocks" he is disparaging may well be trying to be the type of fiduciaries that trust beneficiaries are entitled to; they may properly see their trustworthy service as the heart of the bank's relationship with trust customers; Merrick sees the relationship as "retention selling" of a bank product. The trained fiduciaries properly resist the notion that all trusts should be treated uniformly and dumped into one common trust fund, regardless of its performance and the differing individual investment objectives or needs of the beneficiaries. They may also be uncomfortable about the increasing volume of security transactions of the small trusts, because of the very result that Merrick sees as attractive: more brokerage transactions generate more commissions, and more research from the brokers to the bank generates less research costs for the bank. However, the customer will pay twice for management, through both brokerage commissions and trustee commissions.

Fiduciaries are trained to look at different interests and treat each appropriately. The typical personal trust involves one party entitled to current income and a charity, unborn children, or a relative entitled to the capital at the end of the term. Fiduciaries have to be concerned about unnecessary sales that incur unnecessary capital gains taxes and brokerage commissions as though it were their own money. They must assess the need for these sales and deduce who benefits and who bears the cost. Trust officers weigh these conflicts. Thus, they feel a contradiction if they succumb to Merrick's pressure to consolidate the small trusts into a pooled common trust fund at the cost of commissions and capital gains taxes, for the purpose of saving operations expenses for the bank. Merrick mentions better investment performance, but achieving better performance is tricky. In general, performance can be increased only by employing better (more costly) investment professionals, incurring greater risk, decreasing diversification, selecting stocks with higher volatility, or looking at shorter term horizons. Since Merrick doesn't refer to better investment personnel, the only available tools may involve increased risk. Merrick's desire to get the performance numbers up in order to benefit Midwest's marketing department implies a disregard for any extra risks that would be borne by customers who, being uninformed or dead, won't complain. In contrast, the trust officers are trained and employed to watch out for the uninformed. Yet they are in a weak competitive position. In the eyes of the bank's management the trust department is a cost center in a bank that wants profit centers.

Merrick's ethical blind spot is the trust department's very mission. He simply sees the bank's fiduciary responsibilities as a business problem. Midwest doesn't have to lose money on the trust business in order to be ethical. If it loses money it will cease to be viable and ethical; however, the starting point for an ethical solution has to be rooted in the continued fiduciary allegiance of the bank to the interests of the trust beneficiaries. Only after those interests have been identified is it time to solve Midwest's profit problem.

Merrick comes across as a practical (yet crass) person who is not concerned with intellectual abstraction. Curiously, this profile offers an ethical window. In order to put the bank first he has naively set the bank's self-interest ahead of the customer's interest. The issue can be reframed, tieing the bank's self-interest to customer satisfaction. True, beneficiaries tend not to file complaints: they do not see what goes wrong or they do not know what to do about their grievances, although they may bad-mouth the bank. If there is a germ of ethics in Merrick we may nudge him toward a clearer recognition of the selfish reasons for being ethical about the interest of the beneficiaries.

Merrick's lack of guidance in setting the correct priorities indicates an ethical gap in senior management's understanding. Assuming that this gap is due to a lack of training rather than a deliberate devotion to impropriety, would it help the organization as a whole toward better decisions to issue a written code of ethics and a statement of policy? Such a stated policy for trust services might read:

> We offer a special fiduciary service through our trust department by looking first and foremost to the interest of the beneficiary. A high level of integrity is needed to perform this task and our training and supervision procedures are designed to ensure that the interests of the beneficiaries come first. Under our system of decentralized decisions we rely on trained and informed

professionals who know the client and who can most effectively carry out this commitment.

Had that been the stated (and enforced) policy of Midwest, Merrick would have had an easier time when it came to analyzing ways to make the trust department profitable. The statement sets priorities but does not exclude the bank's interest in receiving a reasonable profit for performing the trustee service. In fact, if a beneficiary is to get excellent service, the service provider must be profitable. Had Merrick listed the interests of income beneficiaries, remaindermen, and the bank, in that order and not the reverse, the proper decision might well have been to use the proposed pooled fund, perhaps with a different timetable—any trust with investment objectives and needs consistent with those of the common trust fund could be shifted into the common fund as liquid assets became available so no unneeded brokerage commissions would be incurred. Stocks would not be routinely sold for noninvestment reasons to accelerate the process. More than one common trust fund would, in such a context, have been discussed, perhaps a bond fund and a cash management account as well as a stock fund; such a combination would collectively permit trust officers to diversify investments, using their training and experience in light of the needs of the specific trust's beneficiaries. The end result could have been financially similar to Merrick's proposal, with the obligation to each particular trust being met. The case for raising fees to provide a profit for a proper service would have been attacked directly.

Establishing such a policy statement is a campaign that a caring trust officer, Marion Tolland, might comfortably pursue. In the absence of such a statement, how do portfolio managers who are uncomfortable with their company's actions respond? Questioning Merrick's ethics could jeopardize their careers; thus, heroic activity is unlikely. Is it unethical to press the case for fiduciary management without mentioning ethics? For instance, an external source of authority could be cited properly and powerfully, such as the legal department with its insistence on documented investment objectives, proper diversification of the portfolio, or reasonable brokerage commissions. That is only a start. Negativism is insufficient in this situation; a positive solution must be proposed. To succeed, Tolland, the campaigning trust officer, needs to be a team player and help Merrick achieve the bank's business objective of profitability, yet she must get the customer back into first place.

Banks were once paternalistic when making loans, but not today. A similar business shift away from paternalism cannot occur in trusts since the bank trustee is being paid to act paternally. Merrick needs to recognize that the trust department has a role beyond that of a vendor. In the proposed statement of policy, Midwest represents itself as having as a primary objective the care of the beneficiaries. The statement of policy as a tool presses Merrick to react positively to serve the beneficiaries who lack that knowledge, independence, or methods of protecting themselves. He might be helped to see how reinforcing and supporting the interest of these customers offers a profit opportunity.

When making major operating decisions, managers do not rely solely on their gut feelings. Analysis and documentation must occur. Managers understand when they should retain an expert rather than make an uninformed guess, yet they sometimes define "conscience" as sentimentality in contrast to quantifiable specified objectives. Merrick's professional training is to increase profits, a quantifiable and specific goal. Merrick can be helped to dig deeper than short-term profits. If the opportunity is spelled out, he can select an action that is both procustomer and proprofit. Tolland may nudge him to see service as a business opportunity. If Merrick acknowledges his limited sensitivity to the social role played by trust officers, he will rely on the judgments of trained fiduciary personnel in their areas of special competence. He will also be working to achieve a three-part goal: be fair to the beneficiaries, increase bank profits, and help his career.

If the bank's chief operating officer is myopic to the customer obligation, Merrick's ethical career opportunity may be to reposition the bank and provide a hook for a new marketing campaign for trust services by drafting a statement of corporate objectives. From the bank's point of view the atmosphere should encourage truthful statements with a goal of effective and reasoned consensus and a minimum of rationalization. There should be no penalties for a specialist whose personal views differ from the group's. Life is too short and the flow of information and competition too rapid to permit anything from blocking the best possible decision. Accurate but careful communication from the trust officer to the bank in terms she is comfortable with, and which the bank will understand and be likely to act on, is important.

Merrick has cast himself in the role of a hot "knowledge worker" with his HP-70 and Lotus 1-2-3 as principal tools. He is proposing to retain the trappings of the trust department while he alters its character. Ethics do not demand (or suggest) that Midwest keep managing an unprofitable division in an unprofitable way: the Midwest shareholders also have rights and are entitled to look for profitable employment of their assets. But to do so properly requires a high caliber of awareness and the prioritizing of interests throughout the process.

Chapter 4

On and Off the Fast Track
Means and Ends

Our friend Merrick's approach to the trust department question fits the initial impression he made at the bank. Scripting more details: he had worked for a management consulting firm while studying for his MBA. He joined the loan department of Midwest after graduation, where his first initiative involved the threat of a forced takeover by Mass Conglomerates of one of the companies whose loans he supervised, a company we will call Deer Field Tool. The head of the loan department gave Merrick his blessing for helping the customer, and provided back-up coverage for Merrick's other responsibilities within the department, allowing him to devote all his energy to the project during the acquisition battle. Merrick on camera:

> That battle was brutal. MassCon made an S.E.C. filing that they had acquired 5 percent of the stock of my customer, Deer Field Tool. And they had to explain their plans, but they didn't tell us much. They said the acquisition was for "investment." We all knew better than that. They wanted control.
>
> I read everything I could find about Deer Field and about the raider, Mass Conglomerates. It was clear that MassCon saw Deer Field's local operations as a source of cash: after they took over they expected to close down the local operations, sell off inventory and patents, and come out ahead. We would lose the customer and get nothing out of MassCon. The question was how we could keep Deer Field afloat.
>
> I had studied some of these things in graduate school and read a lot in the papers about tender offers and takeovers. So I really jumped into the middle of it. The company and the bank both gave me their support and I recommended to the treasurer of

Deer Field that management be issued a new class of convertible preferred stock with fifty votes a share, on any acquisition proposal, so they would have a really big vote. Deer Field lawyers said that was all right and also cleared my idea that Deer Field contribute some of that preferred stock to us as trustee of their pension fund instead of making the annual cash contribution. That was to add more votes and free up cash to use against MassCon. Marion Tolland, who managed the trust investments, put up some static about taking the preferred, but Midwest has a very solid legal department and they are up-to-date on all the government regulations. They cleared it all.

Then Midwest lent money to the key executives to make it easy for them to buy Deer Field stock on the market. What a combination that was. It really slowed MassCon down and we were able to take some more steps then because we had more time: stock options to the executives, some purchases in the public market of Deer Field common by the pension fund. We got the union fund for the hourly workers in the act, too. It was all very exciting. As I guess you know from reading the paper at the time, we won. MassCon got 20 percent of the stock by the end of the battle but that was about it.

They didn't have the votes and they sold their shares, took their losses, and moved on to other targets.

We'd shown how an imaginative and ethical bank can help the client, and that word really gets around.

The management at Midwest recognized and rewarded Merrick's single-mindedness in helping its commercial customer stay independent, focusing the attention of the bank on how to keep the raider from depriving Deer Field managers of their jobs and the bank of its customer. Merrick was imaginative in his work, finding a way to increase prospective votes in a proxy fight by causing the pension fund to invest in a new issue of Deer Field shares and by making the needed line of credit available to the executives for purchasing stock on the open market based on the credit standing of Deer Field and on the pension relationship. We don't know whether the interest rate was especially favorable to the executives, but one can infer that possibility. While he did not discuss whether the preferred stock was appropriate for pension fund investment, we can conclude from Tolland's opposition that the stock was not freely marketable.

How could Merrick have taken ethical values into account and analyzed these issues in a less bumptious and more sophisticated way? Can ethical analysis be systemized? Traditional systems of ethical analysis often seem overly abstract, even to managers with graduate degrees. However, we make use of them in our daily lives. Merrick, as an instinctive utilitarian, would probably find it consistent with his other practices to identify the several constituencies affected by his pending decisions. His primary focus has been on the management of Deer Field and the management of Midwest. Clearly there are other interests, some with a higher ethical priority. Has he looked adequately at the interest of the bank's own shareholders? In this transaction their capital is at risk in several ways. Apart from the potential loss of a major customer, there are significant liability risks in connection with bringing the unmarketable preferred into pension funds, and lending money to the key executives, especially if based on the pension fund relationship. Merrick's specific comments about the bank's legal department indicate the attitude that professional responsibilities do not transcend a legal minimum. Of course, he needs to learn that what is "legal" may or may not achieve the level of "ethical" fairness required to make society work.

In dealing with the pension fund's involvement, Merrick behaved like a general giving orders to his army. He failed to see that the army belonged to Deer Field's pension beneficiaries, not to Deer Field's management. Acting as surrogate management, Merrick pushed the portfolio manager of the pension fund, Marion Tolland. What should her response have been? It is doubtful that she would have had the gall to tell Merrick his suggestion was unethical. Nevertheless, without losing her audience she could have made constructive and professional suggestions: since the new preferred would not be marketable, the bank, before accepting it, should have discussed the subject with the company and documentation that the price had been arrived at after reviewing similarly available issues of the same quality should have been prepared for the bank. Moreover, if Midwest had issued the proposed statement of pro-customer policy, Tolland would be consulted as a fiduciary expert and could have helped address the technical questions whether or not the transfer by the corporation of its new preferred stock to its pension fund was in fact for the "exclusive benefit" of the pension beneficiaries. In both cases the pension fund might have accepted the preferred; however, only in the revised version would control have been in the hands of a knowledgeable and professional on-the-spot team.

Is there a way to know which conflicts of interest are worth worrying about? It is easy to list some of the groups impacted by the bank's actions with respect to Deer Field. That is a good start.

I. The pension fund and beneficiaries
  Current workers
  Vested workers
  Retired workers
  Workers' families
  Future workers
II. Deer Field
  Top management
  Shareholders
  Employees
  Community
III. The raider
IV. The bank itself

It appears that Merrick did not focus on the existence of these different groups, their varied needs and expectations, and the duties owed to them. He just "gave the word" to the trust department to take the preferred stock. But a good manager recognizing Tolland's professionalism would have included her in the process, allowing her to guide the analysis, help establish the principles, and ensure that their application to the specific proposal made sense.

With the benefit of hindsight we can see how Merrick and Tolland might have discussed the maze created by the situation with the intent of establishing conflicts and priorities:

Tolland: We must spell out the interest of the pension fund in the transaction. The risks and opportunities belong to the pension beneficiaries, not to Deer Field's management.
Merrick: Well, MassCon might terminate the pension fund.
Tolland: We don't know that and maybe should explore the point.
Merrick: Makes sense to me.
Tolland: Does Deer Field have the capacity to pay the pension benefits, even if the pension fund's investments are wiped out?
Merrick: Yes, as of today.
Tolland: Then the risk to the employees of the plan taking the preferred stock is considerably less. But what if Deer Field at some future time does not have an independent capacity to pay the pension benefits? The beneficiaries have to look to us as trustee of the plan's assets and they better be good.
Merrick: On a strictly objective basis, what is the risk of taking

in Deer Field stock? Would we buy Deer Field commercial paper on our own?

Tolland: Clearly not. The quality is not high enough.

Merrick: But the preferred is better than nothing. What if Deer Field did not contribute to the fund this year? And what about the loss of jobs if MassCon's raid is successful?

Tolland: You need to separate the interests of the beneficiaries and their retirement benefits from the current block of employees whose jobs would be most likely affected. There is probably a lot of overlap, but the nuances are different. Who are the potential beneficiaries?

Merrick: I don't know. A lot of them are young with years of work ahead. The computer could give us a profile and where the loss of vested benefits would fall.

Tolland: Even if we agree that taking the preferred stock is all right, you talk about actually going out and buying Deer Field stock in the marketplace.

Merrick: The price will probably go up.

Tolland: Because of the takeover! But will the price stay up over the long term? We have to ask if this is a fair price to pay and if we will be able to sell at a profit after this unusual environment is over.

Involving others in a decision often makes practical sense. If we view our own skills and limitations realistically, we will realize that discussion with peers is usually essential in order to fully understand a situation. Merrick and Tolland could speak with a member of the pension committee of the Deer Field board, gaining the views of a person who sees the practical importance of protecting the fund and who has been schooled in the distinction between short- and long-term pressures. True, such a person is also under coercive pressures to protect jobs. But such a person is a potential ally in reaching a balanced decision and is likely to look for a way of protecting the company that does not threaten the pension fund.

In order to reach a fairly balanced decision, a definition of responsibilities is also required. At what point should Midwest, acting as trustee, question the direction given by Deer Field management to accept stock in lieu of cash? Of course, Merrick has initiated these proposals, adding momentum that is harder to correct. But as that sage philosopher Yogi Berra said, "It ain't over 'til it's over!" What if Deer Field had simply said, on its own, that it was transferring the preferred in lieu of cash. How should the bank have responded? Is the problem identical? The bank is responsible for prudent management of the pension fund, but it does not have to solve all of the world's other problems. Does such a transfer affect the bank's obligation to manage the fund, or is this outside its core of responsibility? Should it consider saying, "No, thank you?"

A political way for Tolland to get into the act in the absence of an invitation and a trust department policy statement is for her to speak professionally and specifically to Merrick about her concerns, since she is his superior in fiduciary experience and knowledge, if not on the table of organization. For example, she could send the following memorandum to Merrick:

> The bank's interest in protecting Deer Field against the unfriendly takeover is important to us all. There are many ways in which the interests of the employees and management of Deer Field come together. However, there are different interests in the pension fund, and the U.S. Labor Department is concerned that the funds be managed in the sole interest of the beneficiaries.
>
> Pension fund investments must be reviewed and documented. One matter of fiduciary concern is the proposed transfer by the company of unmarketable preferred stock. There are significant valuation questions, especially in light of the bank's current rating of Deer Field's credit. As you know, the decision has been made to exclude its commercial paper from use by Midwest trust customers. If the preferred is transferred to the Deer Field trust it may be necessary for the trust department to exclude it from our fee and to act only under the directions of Deer Field. In any event, we may have a responsibility to watch over the preferred and need to evaluate risks and opportunities.
>
> In addition, similar situations have invited court orders that block the trustee from voting company stock on a merger question.

This kind of approach avoids a treatise on ethics, expresses Tolland's "team spirit" concern for Deer Field's independence, and touches on understandable risks of criticism of the bank without being false to her conviction. Or is it false? The line must be drawn between effective communication (which requires words the listener understands) and lies, whether the goal is or is not good—unethical means are not justified by good goals.[IV-1]

Justifying the Means and the End

It is not enough to say that the greatest good for the greatest number is derived from the free operation of individual self-interest.

Ethical pragmatists do not base action on self-interest, whether or not the economic theory of the net social good of aggregated self-interest is valid. In order to be ethical, the management must make conscious decisions in light of the probable social good.

The Deer Field pension committee could conclude that the practical result of the preferred stock transfer would promise the best results for all interested persons, including trust beneficiaries, employees, and management. Tolland may agree, yet feel uncomfortable because of the precedents that are being created; if Deer Field can place new unmarketable issues with a pension fund without a word from the trustees, it may encourage other pension fund sponsors to transfer unmarketable securities of questionable value, which would be bad for Midwest. The fact that one action is within the area of propriety may make it difficult to block a similar situation that seems slightly over the line of impropriety. The pension committee says the proposed act is itself ethical; Tolland says the ethical "rule" should prohibit such transfers. Each is consistent with utilitarian concepts, and either road is on relatively high ethical ground.

Merrick's starting point is quite different, of course. If the self-interest of the bank were his sole test, it would be virtually impossible for Merrick to consider the more far-reaching effects. He does not need to be schooled in the more abstract areas of rules and precedents in order to be ethical. He probably doesn't cheat in tennis and is kind to animals; he needs to include such values in his job as a professional manager. As a pragmatist he will understand the benefit of relying on experts for issues where such expertise is required and see that his limited knowledge and experience in the fiduciary field acquires complementary skills. In turn, his legitimate concern with costs can be taken into account in alternatives developed by Tolland.

A Moral Perspective

In 1955, Judge George Frankenthaler, then Surrogate of the County of New York, stated as his biblical credo: "Do justice, love mercy, walk humbly." Justice, rights of others, self criticism.

Although justice is abstract, it has objective guidelines. It is also contextual, intimately tied to the situation in which the decision occurs. Justice involves the effect a particular action, decision, or policy has on others. The actions by Deer Field management, for example, would affect the takeover plan by the raider—at least Deer Field hopes so. They assume it is ethical to interfere with the raider's intentions. But we do not know enough about the facts to be sure. If maintaining Deer Field's independence is of great importance, are all means of doing so ethically proper? Would it be proper for Deer Field to bring pressure upon MassCon's suppliers? To invent a lawsuit in order to break the momentum of MassCon's assault? To threaten personal harm to MassCon principals? To threaten their reputations? While this sounds like yellow journalism, we do know that such aggressive actions have been taken in the passion of the moment. Much of this is unethical. The concept of justice is like a flashing red light warning us to analyze first and act second. It helps for the analysis to be in writing so that we may seek a conclusion using the facts, and have as a goal that the decision be fair.

Merrick and Tolland together could have pursued different ways of analyzing the problem, recognizing that there is no code with a single specific and ethical answer to every problem. Different results and different conclusions for the same factual situation are ethically possible. This is acceptable if managers have identified and spelled out superior alternatives. It is light years ahead of what happened in the Merrick story and on much better ethical ground than actions that are taken because of a "warm internal feeling."

Chapter 5

Whose Vote?
Conflicts of Interest/Conflicts of Perception

We talk in absolute terms of shareholders as the owners of a corporation and ritualize the annual shareholders' meeting, but forget that ownership of anything is an assortment of rights, often held by different people—possession, management, the right to sell, and the right to give away. We own our shoes. We and a mortgage bank may own a house. We and a landlord and a bank may "own" an apartment. When we speak of the public corporation and the rights of shareholders there are many different "slices of ownership." Strategic planning cannot work if we don't accurately assess our starting point.

The profile of shareholders in major U.S. corporations has changed radically since the 1930s when political scientists Berle and Means addressed the policy vacuum created by the concentration of ownership in the hands of passive and unsophisticated individual shareholders, many of whom inherited control stock from entrepreneurial ancestors.[1-2] The vacuum was, of course, filled by responsible people on the spot, the managers. Today institutional shareholders are dominant, have access to a breadth of information, and, at least in trades, are extremely active. But for antitrust, financial, regulatory, efficiency, and political reasons, institutional investors and their intermediaries have been reluctant to play more than a spectator's role in the affairs of the corporation in which they invest. Political activists infer lethargy from such inaction, or even a deliberate abdication of fiduciary responsibility by such institutions. However, many activists would complain even more vehemently if bank trustees and other professional intermediaries were seen to intervene for improper reasons.

The criticism of institutional passivity is most often directed toward the practice of routinely endorsing corporate management proposals at annual shareholders' meetings. Since the 1950s, the Gilbert Brothers, Wilma Soss, Evelyn Davis, and other so-called "corporate gadflies" jousted with managements, suggesting, for example, cumulative voting rights enabling a minority of shareholders to cast all of its votes for a single nominee, rather than a fraction for each, and thus acquire minority representation on boards of directors. They regularly backed other losing proposals including preemptive rights authorizing existing shareholders to purchase new issues of securities before the public and a requirement that the location for the annual shareholders' meeting be shifted around the country to help increase two-way communication between shareholders and management. These mainstream shareholder proposals tended to be automatically rejected by the various "street name" nominees, both banks and brokers, who were comfortable with the "Wall Street Rule" on proxy voting: either support management or sell the stock. One rationale: if each issue had to be voted on after a thoughtful review, the result would have been expensive and chaotic, delays would occur because of a lack of quorum for the necessary meeting, and a subsequent remailing by the corporation needed to resolicit the shareholders in order to achieve a quorum. And all of this would occur when the vote was foregone.

The game changed when headline issues were presented for discussion—issues that had little bearing on the usual business of the corporation but impinged on the public policy attitudes of many institutional investors. Trade unions began to press pension funds to invest in prounion companies; church organizations sought to block drug companies from risking harm to unsophisticated Third World consumers; environmentalists demanded that "Spaceship Earth" be given a voice in the way natural resources are consumed. These issues do not lend themselves to the rationale of the "Wall Street Rule." They are beyond the expertise available to a brokerage firm's proxy desk, or even to a sophisticated investment manager's research department. They are often equally beyond the scope of comfort, knowledge, and skill of the management of the corporation in question. They are not issues that can be quantified and given a dollar cost and benefit. They are "social responsibility" issues with which philosophers, theologians, ethicists, political scientists, and sociologists are apt to be more at home than any hired financial experts. And they will disagree among themselves. Indeed, voting on them is closer to voting for a president of the United States than to selecting a stock based on price and earnings projections. So viewed, it would seem ethically overreaching for the institution to cast its customers' vote at all. Ideally, the vote should come from the beneficial owner. But that is rarely practical. Proxies arrive three or four weeks before a stockholders' meeting takes place. They go to the owner of record, often the bank's or broker's "street name" nominee. After the analysts review the proxy and look at the business issues, only a few days remain to return the proxy to the corporation. If the client is a pooled fund (pension trust, mutual fund, etc.) and one wishes the ultimate investors to express their views on the social responsibility vote, the communication and mechanical problems are virtually insurmountable.

Issues concerning the governing machinery of corporations can be equally complex and have a significant financial impact. They also demand a breadth of knowledge beyond that of a single company or industry. In 1980 when he was chairman of the Securities and Exchange Commission, Harold Williams issued a call to arms by shareholders urging more participatory governance of corporations. That suggestion was receiving some general discussion when low prices of many stocks triggered the current "Star Wars" battles between corporate raiders and their acquisition targets. New governance proposals specifically designed to block unfriendly takeovers in turn blossomed at the hands of management.

To our case. Consider the following response from a trust officer at Midwest, Frederic Dalton, concerning his and his colleagues' responsibilities and actions.

I'm glad to talk about ethics and how I vote our proxies. Of course it isn't really my full-time job. My main job is trust administration.

Here on the personal trust side of the bank we do the voting ourselves. It used to be routine. Ten years ago a ribbon clerk could do it. You just stamped the card and sent it back. Sometimes an officer would take the proxy cards with the vote on them along to the annual meeting so he could make some brownie points with the company. You know: show how big the bank's holdings were so he would have a leg up in seeing a senior officer over there at the corporation the next time he needed some information or wanted to make a sales pitch for a new product. But our holdings are public information now. The S.E.C. requires us to file that information. So we just mail the proxies in like everyone else, instead of bringing them to the meeting.

The issues have also changed a lot. The issues that shareholders are interested in, I mean. It started during the Vietnam War when some peace activists urged Dow Chemical to stop making napalm. When Dow didn't say yes, they went to the S.E.C. staff to get the proposal on the agenda of the stockholders' meeting so that they would get press coverage. When the S.E.C. turned them

31

down, they went to court and got some congressmen all stirred up on the issue, too. The S.E.C. staff found a formula: if the proposal were tied into the business of the target company, for example by being framed as a proposed charter change or a mandated report to shareholders, the proposal would be deemed appropriate for the shareholders' meeting despite opposition of management, whereas the abstract proposition would not be.

Eventually all sorts of political issues were on the proxy ballots— to ban the use of nuclear energy, to ban the company from doing business in South Africa, to ban the company from defense contracts. Then the right-wingers got into the picture with their own set of issues like banning business with the Soviets. Not that the conservative issues ever became really big, but it just shows that it was a politically motivated media effort rather than having very much to do with business.

You can see what a change there was from the old days. When the Gilbert Brothers were active the proxies didn't bother us because we had the "Wall Street Rule" about voting for management. You sold the stock if you didn't like the management or you voted for management and stayed with the company. After all, what is the point of investing in a management unless you are going to support their decisions?

Then suddenly political issues were coming in from everywhere. Not just preemptive rights to buy new issues and cumulative voting on directors, but every imaginable kind of issue. If you could think of it, the next thing you knew you were faced with it on a proxy statement. We started off with the "Wall Street Rule" on these, too.

The corporations were obviously interested in getting our votes. But then we found that some of the insurgents were customers of ours who seemed more interested in these issues than in how well the stock performed. Over in the safekeeping-of-securities department, where we had college endowment fund customers, the problem became a serious priority which they passed over to us to deal with. Lots of these things don't lend themselves to financial analysis. It is more sociology or politics. Whenever there would be a news story about a corporation having a squabble with the community you could bet that there would be a resolution on that subject at the spring shareholders' meeting. So there we were. We couldn't shift the responsibility to a financial analyst who could only do the numbers, and we couldn't vote in favor of management across the board. What with all those trusts we couldn't run a Gallup poll of the beneficiaries, either.

32   The corporation was sometimes the customer of the bank on

the commercial side, too. So we were under extra pressure. Sometimes the corporation's pension fund was a customer or a prospective customer. Sometimes a church group had proposed the resolution and a member of the church was on the bank's own board. Sometimes the trust beneficiary served on the board of a foundation that had strong views. It was a real can of worms and we couldn't get away with abstaining from the votes, although we tried that for a year or two.

So the bank decided to set up a committee and pass the buck on social issues to them. There is a professor (Joanna Buckley from the State University) and a political writer (Sam Browning who is on the Channel 3 Evening News). I act as the chairman.

This is the way it works. If the issue has a significant financial impact in my mind I vote the proxy myself, checking with anyone in the bank who might be helpful. Other issues go to the committee. For example, even on South African issues I call a research analyst and find out the profit and loss from the South African operation. Usually it is very little and that issue then comes to the committee. Or, maybe a better example would be the cost to an aerospace company if it were to be prohibited from doing business with the U.S. Defense Department: that would be right at the heart of earnings. Anyway, the nonfinancial issues, the social issues, I outline the issue and my recommendation in a little memo to my writer and professor. They agree or disagree and that's that—a majority vote carries unless one of us asks for a meeting on it. We meet three or four times a year anyway, just to go over how the proxy season is unfolding.

The system works as we hoped. If the bank has a customer who disagrees with how we vote we are able to explain our system of committee independence. If the company is knocking at our president's door lobbying for our vote, he agrees the committee will look at any materials they give us. It's a lot better than any other system I've been able to think of.

There is another benefit of the committee. We tell those that ask us to vote for them that this is all confidential and that we will not give out the way we actually voted.

The company certainly can trace the information because they know the name of the bank nominee, but the question usually stops when we explain that the committee welcomes any information that we receive. On a couple of the really hot issues, we have actually met with one side or the other and heard them out. That is unusual, though, because of our size I generally get some special lobbying a dozen or more times a year.

We have developed this checklist that I complete and circulate to the committee for each shareholders' meeting that has contested issues on the agenda:

Significance to the company. To what extent is the company involved?

For example, if the proxy proposes adding antipollution equipment to the factories, what is the company doing now, and how much would new costs be against any possible savings until regulation catches up?

Harm; to whom and how much. What harm is being claimed?

For example, on the use of nuclear power, is there a risk to a nearby community?

We are helped on details by a proxy service we subscribe to from the—Investor Responsibility Research Center—I.R.R.C. in Washington, D.C. They spell out the different arguments on an issue and provide the documentation we need. Each member of the committee gets a set of materials. And that is a pretty good answer when some partisan pushes hard.

Who is the sponsor? Who is proposing the resolution?

For example, is it a believable shareholder with a significant stake in the company or just some outsider with ten shares looking for publicity?

What is the cost of compliance? How expensive would it be for the company to comply with the resolution?

For example, does the resolution say the company ought to abandon a plant? Or is the proposal simply to report to the public data that are already available internally and easily transposed? Even there you have to be careful that the company isn't being asked to give up confidential information or something that would hurt it competitively.

The bank's customers. What have we heard from them; is there a specific effect on our community?

For example, sometimes an issue would not cost the company very much money overall, but could have a large effect on the bank's customers and on the bank itself.

Recently, there has been a new set of considerations. These are the so-called corporate governance issues. For instance, should women directors be required? Should a minority of shareholders have a right to get a representative on the board? Should there be a member from the union? Or a person, such as a professor, who doesn't have any ties to the company? In a sense these are like the old Gilbert Brothers issues but they come from both sides: managements are also pushing a lot of governance points in order to protect their companies from unfriendly takeovers or to ensure continuity of management.

Right now we have a governance issue that I am finishing up. It is a so-called "shark repellent." The management of Forth Right Financial is proposing to move its state of incorporation to Delaware. A new holding company in Delaware would acquire the business of Forth Right. The Delaware statute lets a company limit the rights and powers of shareholders more than other states, and the Delaware corporation would issue privately new preferred stock that would have power to veto a merger or acquisition. Our customers hold a fair amount of the stock and Margaret Andrews, our analyst, is mumbling about lost takeover opportunities, but agrees that Forth Right has good managers who have done well by the shareholders. Earnings have continued to increase and the stock price has gone up, too.

Going down the checklist:

Significance cuts both ways.
This new preferred can help a good company protect itself. Here you cannot quantify what the takeover opportunities are. Forth Right isn't in the oil business where T. Boone Pickens is around the corner, ready to push the stock price up.
Harm. The harm seems remote.
The *sponsor* is a responsible management.
Cost. The management says the cost is reasonable.
The bank's customers. Forth Right is not a customer of the bank, at least not yet, but I got a call today from our new business development office saying it is now a pension fund prospect. We haven't had much new business like that for a while and it is a really big fund.

The New York Stock Exchange had a rule in this area for a while. I guess they still have it, but you don't hear much about it; a small group of shareholders shouldn't have a vote that would override the vote of the common stockholders. But that position hasn't been particularly developed.

It isn't as though there is anything illegal about which way you vote on any of this. In fact, if you think it through, the long-term shareholder who wants to stay with Forth Right is probably not served very well by an unfriendly acquisition. The company's

35

regional network would just get swallowed up by any takeover raider. So I have recommended that we vote for the management. My memorandum will be simple to write—all I have to do is look at the points I.R.R.C. views as favorable.

I suppose there are about fifteen issues concerning different companies with pending shareholder meetings that arrived on my desk this week. With the checklist, I will be able to get the whole package out today, so you can see how our system provides prompt, ethical decision making.

Dalton knows his subject and the conclusion Dalton reaches on Forth Right is coherent, but there are some flashing red lights to check out.

Of all the ethical tensions, the one we are most accustomed to dealing with is the resolution of conflicting claims, including our own claims. While we probably don't spend a great deal of time thinking about it, we do balance the interests of others against our own interests, occasionally overruling our own interests. Sidney Weinberg during his long tenure as senior partner at Goldman Sachs pointed out in a Congressional hearing that conflicts of interest exist for everyone in every life role. We can think of such relationships as God and country; spouse and children; job and family; Daniel Webster's "one and inseparable, liberty and union, now and forever;" the New Haven motto "for God, for country, and for Yale." Yet we unconsciously balance such conflicting perspectives in a workable way every day without much discomfort. As managers also, we routinely balance the conflicting claims of those affected by our decisions. We should look twice, however, when our intuitive conclusion supports our self-interest. We can kid ourselves about our own impartiality and about our grasp of the specifics involved. We must examine our reasoning and test our conclusion: are we really just rationalizing a conclusion we already reached in our own favor?

So, the first question for Dalton concerns the competing claims he must sort out. A key factor in this situation is that the beneficiaries of Midwest trusts who own Forth Right stock rely on the experience and disinterestedness of Midwest for protection. It is "their" shares the bank is voting. The possible harm or benefit to the beneficiaries of the trusts from a vote for or against the new preferred seems somewhat remote and obscure from what Dalton told us. But we don't know whether this proposal is going to turn out to be a timely change blocking an imminent tender offer. All things being equal, it is difficult to see why a bank that functions as a trustee would develop a sentimental attachment to a stock whose upside price is artificially limited. Moreover, common sense tells us a corporate management tends to take this type of action only when a practical benefit (viz, blocking unfriendly assaults) is in sight. And we must not forget that the bank wants the Forth Right pension business.

The trust beneficiaries cannot be asked to fend for themselves. By contract the beneficiaries have a priority claim on the energy and skill of Midwest. Practically speaking they are probably not well enough informed even if they care, and Midwest will not hear from them no matter which way it votes; practically speaking, the bank's employment as trustee tends to be permanent, so the pressure to do a good job in order to retain the customer is not high.

The bank's concept of solving such problems through outside expert participation on the proxy committee is quite appealing. Instead of trying to "legislate" all the positions needed in the future or making individual decisions that reflect only its own views, the bank is relying on "three wise experts" for the construction of guidelines and the application of these guidelines to the facts. So far so good.

The bank is responsible for voting. The bank needs a human agent, in this case the trust officer. This has been expanded to the committee of independents, at least in part, to insulate the bank from criticism. There is a question of what the qualifications of the independents should be, but the mix here makes sense. Practically speaking, a qualified ad hoc group can't be put together on each issue. So there must be a diversity of talents plus enthusiasm. The committee could, of course, add an outside resource person when that seems useful. In any event, the simple efficiency of the current plan should be preserved at all costs.

Members should be chosen by the bank rather than by a self-perpetuating committee. The bank has the responsibility and the committee is designed to assist the bank. If a committee appointment is for a term, there is pressure on the committee to suit the bank's views. If appointments are permanent there is a cozy relationship, too. Perhaps a term without reappointment increases the independence. But then you lose experience and good people. How the committee should vote relates to issues like the Forth Right conflict. Maybe the bank person should only break a tie, leaving to the independents the usual vote. A sociologist and a journalist are a good combination.

We don't know how the experts were chosen, what their ties are to Midwest, or how much value they add. Even assuming that the committee has substantive importance and that they have both authority and competence, it is theoretically preferable to shift to a closer representative of the beneficiary—the individual cotrustees— when possible. This classifies the experts as a committee of last resort. Yet even if theoretically possible and desirable, the idea may be overridden by the practicalities of the cost.

The last issue on the checklist really relates to disqualification of the bank. Consensus among the experts works only if there is an open dialogue. In this case the new business pressure can warp Dalton's judgment; whether the pressure comes from himself, the new business officer, or the management of Forth Right may not matter. There is a distortion of some sort, which is very hard for any employee to sort out and discount. By participating in the proxy decision Dalton is manipulating his committee. There is probably a past base of goodwill built up that gives Dalton's views a special weight. Under the circumstances, however, his views should be given much less weight than usual.

Dalton is in command. The starting recommendation in this case is to support management in its proposed shift to Delaware and proposal for a new stock issue. In addressing the self-interest concern should Dalton disclose the prospective relationship between the bank and the Forth Right fund? Is that enough? Depending on the sophistication of the committee colleagues this disclosure may cause them to feel uncomfortable if they fail to support him, believing that Dalton would feel his own personal integrity was being questioned. Would it be better for Dalton to abstain, indicating a conflict without implying in which direction the conflict would prompt the bank? Rather than admitting that there is a possible customer relationship with Forth Right that may create a conflict of interest, he need simply attach the I.R.R.C. report and explain that he is not making a recommendation because of unspecified potential conflicts of interest. Thus, the precedent of abstention for future conflict of interest situations is built.

If this approach is novel, Dalton should consider the prospective reaction by the bank—and the sales department. Should he anticipate a challenge for following a procedure like that on his own? If so, one course of action would be to talk to Buckley and Browning, focusing their attention on how to handle such situations, inviting them to recommend and then vote on a policy of abstention by any member whenever there is self-interest. If there is subsequent back-biting at the bank, the existence of such a formal procedure would help protect his career, continue his responsibility on the job, and assist his successor to do the same in the interest of the beneficiaries.

A more fundamental question is whether the committee as constituted is competent to review corporate governance issues. Unlike *corporate social responsibility* questions, *governance* issues like this can significantly affect the value, price, and marketability of the stock. As they require financial analysis, such issues are more within the body of the professional expertise of a security analyst than of a sociologist. It is, however, unrealistic to expect that Margaret Andrews, a financial industry security analyst assigned by the bank to Forth Right, is also trained to evaluate the proposed preferred and the shift to Delaware, both specifically and as a precedent for other situations. But her comments should not be disregarded. Without shifting responsibility to trained analysts, Dalton remains the key person. It would seem essential that Andrews be asked for a memorandum that could go to the other members of the committee.[V-1] To ask her for information at this late date could be tricky unless the request is limited to a list of pros and cons rather than a recommendation. She, of course, is also subject to diversionary pressures, including self-interest of the bank in procuring a new customer. A call from the sales manager that pushes her toward a particular result can be as coercive as the call to Dalton. A rule that states "abstain where there is a relationship" should be applicable to both Dalton and Andrews.

Is there any other information we need? In Act II we learn more about the adequacy of Dalton's *"Reader's Digest"* summary of the Forth Right proposal. We learn the Forth Right proxy statement includes this reorganization plan:

REORGANIZATION-PLAN—Approve a plan that would make Forth Right Financial a wholly owned subsidiary of a new Delaware company, Forth Right Inc. All shares of outstanding stock of the operating company would be exchanged for equivalent shares of the holding company stock. Forth Right Financial will remain an Ohio corporation. The reorganization facilitates future expansion and diversification of its business activities and a holding company structure will afford greater flexibility and additional financial and business alternatives by permitting a broader choice of financing and organizational approaches.

* * *

We also have entered into agreements with fifteen of our key executives that provide for the following payments in the event that any of them is dismissed within thirty-six months after a change in the control of the company: (1) accrued vacation pay; (2) between two and five times the executive's highest annual base salary as determined by the board; (3) between two and five times of the executive's highest incentive compensation paid during any one of the five years immediately before the change in control or the termination. In addition, upon a change in control, bonuses pending under the company's management bonus plan and awards of stock under the incentive stock option plan would vest immediately. Stock options also would be exercisable immediately upon the change in control.

We propose a new stock option plan to grant key employees incentive and nonqualifying stock options. The company would make available 4 million shares of common stock for the plan. Option prices would be no less than market price at the time of the grant. There are about 300,000 outstanding unexercised options under the existing plan and no new option grants will be made under that plan. The company has approximately 20 million shares of common stock outstanding.

No wonder Andrews was "mumbling over lost opportunities!"

This statement is quite involved and is likely to be difficult for a journalist and a social scientist to evaluate, no matter how informed they are on issues of corporate social responsibility. A plan to seek additional objective business input is essential, especially since there is so much more involved than Dalton provided in his summary—more for management and less for the shareholders.

Chapter 6

Voting on War and Peace
Ultimate Corporate Social Responsibility

Even a suitably expert proxy committee needs to do advance planning and special reading. Meetings in January or February, before the proxy season begins, are desirable so that other experts can meet with the three members of the Midwest committee. The Investor Responsibility Research Center will produce advance information about the issues expected to be on the proxies in the upcoming rash of shareholders' meetings. With that I.R.R.C. input a series of good ground rules can be set for probable votes, so that when the specific resolutions are received the decision is not *de novo*. There can always be a change if the committee concludes that the facts in a particular case warrant a position different from the "model."

Assume that in January the proxy committee adopts a general policy to support shareholder resolutions that would require portfolio companies doing business in South Africa to treat South African employees without regard to race, as spelled out in the principles regarding employment conditions which were developed by Reverend Leon Sullivan, the Baptist minister who serves on the board of General Motors Corporation.[VI-1] Subsequently, resolutions are in fact proposed to close down the South African business operations of two U.S. companies we will call General Mines Inc. (GMI) and Macro Digestibles Corporation on the grounds they had not adopted and implemented corporate policies required by the Sullivan Principles. Research by I.R.R.C. shows that although GMI had not adopted the Sullivan Principles, its corporate policies had been consistent with those policies: a vote in favor of management might be warranted. For Macro, which had adopted but ignored the Sullivan Principles, a vote against management might be indicated. The model is a helpful and efficient guideline in either case.

Of course the bank is not limited to a binary yes/no choice on a resolution. It can also abstain from voting on resolutions.

For example, it can be convinced on an issue in abstract terms but find the language of the resolution too broad, too narrow, off-the-track, or otherwise inadequate. It can abstain in silence or abstain and write a letter expressing its views. Similarly, a vote in favor of a resolution can be clarified by a letter indicating the reasons for the vote and any reservations the bank has; a vote against a resolution may say "we voted 'no' but had the resolution been worded more artfully, we might have gone the other way."

Dalton, our friend from Midwest Trust, asked about complex votes, might describe a recent conflict over weapons production by companies we will call Military Defense Corporation (MDC) and Canfield Electric, as well as his colleagues' reaction.

The resolution proposed to MDC is unusual. Normally peace groups propose that a company get out of nuclear production. But here the resolution directs the board of directors to put together a set of social, economic, and ethical standards for MDC. There are also proposals to mandate reports to stockholders. Reports are not unusual; trying to put the ethical monkey on the back of the directors is new. The focus goes way beyond whether a contract is or is not profitable and raises environmental, employment, and public support issues.

MDC is vehemently against this resolution, making the point that the real purpose of the resolution is to end the important role MDC plays in the defense industry. They review a lot of technical points they have had to address in answering the proposal, and answers are difficult to sort out if you have to vote "yea" or "nay" to each. Management doesn't stop there as you might expect: they go to higher ground and say that they as a company have an "ethical obligation" to utilize their skills to achieve the defense goals established by the U.S. government.

We had no model for this one and I called the other two members of our proxy committee. Over the telephone, Sam Browning argued that MDC was virtually part of the Defense Department and that Congress and the Administration are places to haggle over public policy. After that, MDC or whoever is selected should carry out the national security goals. We in the public shouldn't be second-guessing. We can't have the needed information. You know, Henry Luce and *LIFE* magazine's ideal of "Pax Americana:" for forty years the world has been more stable because of U.S. military strength.

Joanna, Professor Buckley, had a different starting point, and after the call she sent around this memo:

The real reason for our committee is to help the bank make ethical investments as well as a profit for the beneficiaries. We are supposed to bring to bear our own judgments rather than serve as blotting paper for what someone else says. That is also what MDC's management is being asked to do here: make its own good faith judgment on some very important issues. Some of them relate to their own company, some to humanity as a whole. Remember, the German military leaders who tried to say after World War II they shouldn't be held responsible for carrying out the orders of their superiors in connection with the Holocaust? That excuse didn't wash. And shouldn't have. No excuse could justify mass execution of innocent individuals. Now this resolution is saying nuclear weapons may have some good things to be said for them, but they can also wipe out unbelievable numbers of innocent people. These facts have to be balanced not just in Washington but also by the people who voluntarily carry them out.

We should analyze the resolution and address the parts before the whole. These seem to be:

- The percentage of defense work contracted by MDC
- Lobbying Congress and competitive bidding
- The effect on employees and the environment
- Canons of ethical business
- Sales of weapons to foreign governments—percentages and uses
- The ethics of developing these weapons systems

Well, her memo opens up biological, chemical, and "Star Wars" questions, and we could spend the next year discussing it. We could get a writer like Jonathan Schell and a diplomat who has negotiated with the Soviets like Paul Warnke to visit us and still not know! Besides, we didn't have until next year, we had ten days. But Joanna was adamant, said it was a core decision. She was right about the need to review her points.

First, the contracts with the Energy and Defense Departments and all that. MDC has stressed its military and aerospace business. What was the percentage of total revenues there (it was 80 percent), and what were the financial risks of being so dependent on government (they were large)?

Next, lobbying. What about those MDC vice presidents and registered lobbyists located in Washington, D.C.? Should Congress be lobbied to adopt programs that benefit MDC but may be un-   43 necessary or cost the taxpayers too much, risk escalation of the arms race, or involve potential mass destruction? Should the military be lobbied for new weapons or should MDC wait until the Defense Department has made a decision and only then get into the act? Would that hurt them competitively? What about the way they've handled the subcontracts? They had worked it out so subcontractors were in every one of the fifty states. Was that for geographical stability or to put pressure on Congressmen in the key Congressional districts? Is that such a good idea either from the point of view of the world or the integrity of Congress? Is it an answer to say "everyone else does it?" Well, everyone doesn't do it: in fact, we learned that some very good companies such as Honeywell and GE have policies against lobbying for these contracts.

Third, employment is tied to dependency on defense policy and appropriations. One day it is "fat city" and then you open the newspaper the next day and you learn they may have to fire hundreds of people. How do they deal with that? Should a retraining program be mandated and its costs built into the government contracts? Would that proposal put MDC at a competitive disadvantage?

On the environment, there's all that business of Agent Orange and chemicals that stay in the neighborhood forever, and then we even got into the question of dumping hazardous wastes and building on top of them. Like the news reports about Love Canal.

The issue of sales to foreign governments ties into whom you should sell to. How about some dictatorship that beats up on its people.

We learned that some weapons, like poison gas, are barred by international law, but not nukes. That distinction should give us some help in drawing the line between horror and legitimacy but I don't know what it is. We went over basic business ethics— treating employees fairly, having prices that recognize costs and value, honoring agreements with suppliers and customers. At about that time we sold the MDC stock.

We got back to the question almost immediately as a similar resolution was addressed to Canfield Electric and rejected by its management. We want to hold the stock; actually we have been buying it. They are doing very well, could become a prime contractor in "Star Wars" research and deployment and have top-quality management. And there is no question that these proposals involve core business and policy questions: fair pricing, product quality, efficient operations, the canons of good business practice, handling of hazardous wastes, the level of radiation in nuclear work. On employment, the problem of instability and how much of a commitment to make to advance notice of layoffs and job retraining to protect people from sudden and indefinite layoffs. Lobbying for government contracts by citing the jobs created and lost in specific Congressional districts; or advertising the income to local communities. The issues are all in this resolution and are almost all traditional management responsibilities.

The shareholders were proposing not more than one-third of Canfield's total sales be from defense contracts. It is not likely that swords will be hammered into plowshares in my lifetime, but diversity and long-range stability go together. At a different level, military sales to foreign governments charged with serious human rights violations would be banned. The proponents contrast Austria with the U.S. and Soviets. Austria has such a policy but not the U.S. and the Soviets, which account for over two-thirds of total arms exports.

Then they get to weapons of mass destruction—nuclear, chemical, biological—and the impossible-to-answer questions, such as: "Would the process of developing effective "Star Wars" defense systems in space destabilize the situation and accelerate the interim production of offensive weapons so that the targets could be obliterated despite stronger defenses? Perhaps even invite a war while the odds are still favorable?"

It's all a far cry from the simple resolution saying, "Don't harm people." If it is tough for our committee, what do you think it is for the average shareholder? How in the world can you approach resolutions like this?

Dalton is right; the issues seem to be beyond the scope of any of us. Yet in fact, ordinary managers are dealing with them at Canfield. They are taking on contracts, setting up procedures, and worrying about pickets. Perhaps Canfield's opposition to the resolution is superficial, but it is accurate that a set of published guidelines could hurt Canfield competitively, raise questions in the minds of government negotiators about the commitment, and draw continuing press criticism of the inadequacy of their decisions. Shareholders who favor socially responsible actions promote the logic of their position, alerting fellow shareholders to the long-term effects the weapons business can have on humanity as a whole. Of special note here is the proposition that "the health and well-being of the American free enterprise system depends on actors in the system (including corporations) who accept individual responsibility for their programs, policies, and products."[VI-2]

If this is a "vote yes or no" question on the total resolution, the course of least resistance is to vote for management and trust them as the "top" people in Dalton's eyes. Either yes or no seems premature, but regardless of the shareholder vote, each director of Canfield should privately adopt this proposal as a personal checklist of concerns that he or she must address. The proposal in turn suggests a similar level of awareness and concern to be exercised by financial intermediaries.

The constituencies being discussed are stockholders (the value of the stock and its future earnings stream), employees and their families (jobs, health) and humanity (war and peace). Is it enough to allow the government to resolve this question? In *A Man for All Seasons* we get two answers: a successor to the Duke of Norfolk could properly say, "Leave it to the King; as his loyal subject I will give him my best and support that decision." A successor to Thomas More could say, "As the King's loyal subject I must use my own head and give him my best judgment and best action."

A citizen (including a corporation) is not absolutely obligated to support every program that a government deems necessary or desirable. As moral beings, not caricatures out of George Bernard Shaw's imagination, the MDC and Canfield executives should recognize the issue of potential harm flowing from their business decisions. That does not mean endorsing an unattainable sentimental goal of no more suffering in the world, but hardheaded efforts to develop tools and techniques to ameliorate unnecessary harm. Individuals with assigned responsibilities cannot ignore the consequences of their actions, some of which will be harmful. As moral beings, there comes a time when a citizen may be obligated to resist or even violate governmental instructions at personal cost. Is that how Colonel Oliver North saw his responsibility in connection with the support of anti-Sandinista forces in Central America? If so, did he serve his cause well?

It is not a simple matter to go about this in a way that properly uses the mind. It can help to start by acknowledging the parochialism with which we tend to respond to issues that can cause harm: our harm is good harm, we say. This reaction is not limited to nuclear weapons but extends to a one-sided sales campaign whose only harm will be to remove money from unsophisticated consumers for a poor-quality product.

Should the Dalton committee decide on each subsection of the resolution or just the policy? Can it do both? While the resolution is complex and the specifics are hard to wrestle with, the I.R.R.C. Proxy Issues Report on the subject VI-3 can help add clarity. Although it is a long and detailed analysis, it is in plain English and can be understood by a committee. Another practical step is to test the impact on earnings with the analyst for the bank.

How can the proxy committee justify an adequate amount of time to deal with issues of this sort? The time will be paid for by shareholders of the bank. Is the benefit to customers and the share-holders substantial enough to warrant an extensive commitment to the area? In the last analysis, this issue involves balancing the questions of society, government, and business that measure the protection of freedom for the country, a history of forty years without global war tied to the possession of ultimate weapons by the Soviet Union and the United States, the small number of haz-ardous results known to have occurred from nuclear installations and enthusiasm of the Japanese and the French for such installations, and the enormity of harm that is risked. Are the members of this committee much more expert on the ultimate questions than the customer whose money is being invested in Canfield? Certainly the committee can cope with stability-of-employment issues, lobbying, and the philosophic concept that ethical business has a responsibility for just pricing, product control, efficient operations (not wasting public or private funds), truthful advertising, maintenance of a safe workplace, and fair employment procedures.

When time for a new responsibility is made available by neglecting previously assigned responsibilities, relative costs and benefits must be newly weighed. If each proxy issue is to be dealt with in detail, the bank will be under financial pressure to get out of the responsibility entirely. So a balance must be struck. From time to time an issue of seminal importance and strength does need extra study, but I.R.R.C. reports analyze such issues apart from a specific resolu-tion.[VI-4] They can be reviewed at the preseason committee meeting and a reasonable calendar established.

For years there have been individualized investment guidelines in fiduciary operations: if a family is concerned about gambling and alcohol, a directly managed trust excludes casino stocks and liquor stocks, whether or not they are otherwise attractive investments. If the family favors a strong defense establishment, its views on a resolution that prohibits contracts with the Defense Department would not necessarily be better in a professional sense, but would be superior in the sense that family views on political or societal grounds preempt investment decisions. The model and backup in-formation used by the proxy committee might be made available to the individual trustees or to the beneficiaries, so the bank might become only a decision maker of last resort when it came to how the family's interest should be voted.

Broader participation also addresses the hazards of elitism: financial institutions may travel in a pack and impose their own sociopolitical views on society through the proxy machinery and the voting power of their customers' assets. Votes that can significantly affect the value or price of the stock are inherent in the responsibility of a trustee; voting on issues where the shareholders' meeting becomes a forum for social or political argumentation is inherently the investors' responsibility. On political and social issues financial institutions have no blank check to override their customers' views.[VI-5]

Where does all this lead? The adequacy of Dalton's checklist becomes extremely important, featuring "harm"—the effects on people, remote or proximate, serious or ephemeral—as a question. Is MDC's management right in saying the judgment of the government with respect to the necessity of the proposed harmful equipment is final? Is its conclusion entitled to any presumption of accuracy? Does that depend on the reputation of management? Whose harm are we concerned with? In an age that equates TV news simplification with reality, we sometimes miss harm to the unpublicized needy neighbor when identifying more remote groups that need our help; great issues of war and peace can engage attention that would be used more constructively in small but real steps we ourselves take toward or away from a better world.[VI-6] Great harm can be caused by a weak defense system that invites predators; weapons can be used by despots to brutalize their citizens. In choosing its course despite the transcendent threat of nuclear war and its likelihood or unlikelihood, MDC management may be correct. The fact that a company run by a cartoon villain would reach the same conclusion does not make the decision wrong. We want a management that thinks out the dichotomies. We may have no right to ask more of them; we need to ask as much of ourselves.

Perhaps the best result at this stage would have been abstention with an explanation to Canfield that Midwest will develop its own statement of values and corporate purposes and make them available to Canfield; that they urge each Canfield director to develop a list of personal and corporate values. Some values, which directors share privately, may be generally agreed on, but disagreement is part of the process. By identifying rarely articulated values, everyone on the board should be more comfortable in using rationality and common sense in the tricky area of business ethics.

In the effort to systematize the decision beyond a gut feeling, stream of consciousness, and slavish following of analytical logic, the personal integrity of each decision maker at Midwest and Canfield is important. Dalton's personal integrity and that of Browning and Buckley will not provide identical answers: each is tied into personal values and experience. Contradiction must be resolved by concession and negotiation, by persuasion and abdication. At some point loyalty to one's peers should outweigh the obligation to unknown affected persons, but not always, and only if consistent with fairness, relative harm, and the concept of justice. We must be careful not to distort the negotiation by coercing others or by some clever manipulation that affects their jurisdiction over their own lives.[VI-7]

The Dalton committee voted in favor of the Canfield management for the accounts for which the bank had voting power and asked the president of the bank, Mark Vale, to send a letter of clarification to D. D. River, the president of Canfield. The committee also urged that customers who vote the shares themselves receive a similar letter of explanation and a copy of Mr. Vale's letter to Canfield. Vale's reaction follows:

The decision of the proxy committee came as a surprise. Defense is a big issue and really one that bankers can't answer. But Mrs. Buckley's strong point was that this is an opportunity to forestall the government from telling business what we can and cannot do; here the directors can stand up and say, 'I'll be the judge!'

It makes some sense to have the bank communicating with customers invested in Canfield, to demonstrate our interest and the fact that the committee is independent; that we developed it—at our expense I might add—to represent the interests of our customers.

I agreed to send something, but it seemed to me important that the letter be phrased in terms of the committee's views rather than those of the bank management. People will disagree violently with any position we take. I spent time on the letter myself and had the public relations department fuss with it as well. The committee approved the text in the end.

I made the point that we were not challenging the good faith or the business objectives of Canfield. The directors and managers have to be able to work a lot of this out privately with a public statement of corporate policy. The statement could be good P.R. for Canfield as well as answer some of these questions, but details have to be left to the directors and they need time.

We didn't send any copies to the press, but they somehow got hold of a copy of the letter from one of the customers or some dissident at Canfield. Unfortunately, the news story is slanted against Canfield and they are holding it against us.

This is a letter to agency customers who have voting power over the securities:

Dear Customer:

As a holder of Canfield Electric Corporation common stock you are entitled to vote at its annual meeting at the end of this month. We have reviewed the proxy statement and enclose a card signed by us as the shareholder of record. You need only check the boxes that reflect your desires and mail the proxy card in the enclosed stamped, addressed envelope to the Corporation.

There has been submitted to the shareholders a detailed resolution that you can read about in the attached proxy statement and on which I wish to comment.

To assist our customers we established, some time ago, a proxy committee consisting of a noted journalist, a professor of sociology and political science, and a senior bank officer. The committee reviews complicated issues of corporate governance and so-called corporate social responsibility. My letter to the president of Canfield Electric reports on the committee's conclusions; a copy is enclosed.

We hope this service proves helpful to you in your analysis.

The letter from Vale to the president of Canfield is also brief.

Dear Mr. River:

We read with interest your proxy statement for the current shareholders' meeting and enclose proxy cards signed by the bank for those shares where we have direct power to vote. Such cards support the position of the management on all issues coming before the meeting; however, we wish to clarify our point of view.

Some time ago, the bank established an independent committee to advise us on issues of corporate governance and corporate social responsiblity. The committee has asked me to tell you that they believe the proposed ethics resolution contains points that deserve your attention and consideration; if not in the form proposed, at least in some other appropriate manner. Specifically, they recommend that you review the high business standards you have maintained in the past and enumerate them in a published code of ethical business conduct. It is their belief that as you expand into new products the code will help employees and suppliers effectively support those standards of conduct. The code should include the essential element of profit.

The committee considers this resolution an opportunity for Canfield to demonstrate its leadership through encouraging the individual responsibility of directors. They also suggest appointing a committee of your independent directors who will put their "good housekeeping seal of approval" on new products in light of the interest of shareholders, management, workers, and the communities affected.

Are these responsible letters? They do not convey the committee's wide-ranging concerns, although they begin to chip away at the most readily supported area of "ethical business practice" and imply that there is a committee of unleashed watchdogs who will continue to monitor unpleasant developments. By being given to customers, the information has developed some momentum of its own without necessarily destroying the relationship with Canfield. The letters are accurate though deliberately incomplete.

How concerned should we be about apparent pressure put on the proxy committee to achieve a result that is consistent with the interests of the bank rather than the interests of the shareholders, the tension between adequate self-defense and escalation of costs, global risks and unquestioning acceptance of larger military budgets? Public acknowledgement of the proxy committee may increase its independence. So viewed, the committee members may not feel they have been misused. But if they conclude that Vale exceeded the bounds of propriety, resignation should be considered. Resignation is a onetime possibility, but a willingness to resign must be accepted by committee members if they are to remain independent.

Chapter 7

Rooting for the Home Team
Where Do We Draw the Line?

Tender offers pose very tricky problems for financial advisers. Only a few of the issues are quantifiable and even they involve important projections. To help get at the issues we turn to a portfolio manager, Rosalind MacReed. She has spent the last eight years in her firm and is the first woman to be assigned to manage a corporate pension fund. Her comments are directed to actions of Retton and the Motley Group, two companies that are engaged in a struggle for control of Retton.

Now I have several large pension funds but certainly the one that is most interesting at the moment is the retirement fund of M.L. Retton Co., Inc. The performance of the fund has been very competitive over the years I have had it and we have a terrific relationship with the people over at the company. The person in charge gets promoted after about two years on the fund, so we have had several bosses who are now V.P.s but used to be in the controller's office and dealt with us in connection with the mechanics of the fund—actuarial assumption changes, funding requirements, new wrinkles added to the pension plan, etc. I mention it because that puts us in a very good position to help them in a situation as complicated as the request that the public tender its shares to the Motley Group.

All of the tender offers that hit the headlines are unfriendly, otherwise each announcement would be made jointly by the managements of both corporations. No matter what the target company says, it's got to be an upsetting thing for its management. Just before the Motley tender offer hit the papers Retton stock was selling at $42 a share and earning $7 a share. Although the market as a whole has been flat since then, the Retton stock price has moved up to $58, which is where it closed yesterday. The offer is share-for-share, with Motley stock worth $63 a share. That amounts to nine times Retton's last year's earnings—our own internal earnings estimate is for them to earn the same this year.

Motley has had a history of expansion through acquisitions and its earnings have tended to grow erratically. Its own stock has been selling at a premium to earnings in-line with a lot of similar companies. It is certainly no Beatrice Foods, which made hundreds of acquisitions over the last twenty-five years. You could, though, say that Motley's central business is mergers with good companies that have a much lower multiple of earnings. It has worked well but there have been no dramatic hits.

On the other hand, Retton may have too much of a commitment to the status quo. I don't mean that they are 100 percent closed to new ideas, new products, and new distribution approaches, but they are generally reluctant to terminate a product or a division. They always find some reason for continuing to manufacture and distribute products that were once successful but aren't now, so long as the product has a continued band of loyal customers, however small.

Well, with that kind of situation, how should we answer Motley's tender offer? The Retton Salaried Employees Retirement Trust has held 10 percent of its outstanding stock for many years. Another thing, many of our trusts hold Retton shares—which comes to another 7 percent; some were inherited and some bought at our suggestion.

My specific assignment is to decide whether to accept the offer. Obviously we could tip the balance of the war in favor of Motley if we were to tender our stock. I don't think anyone at the company thinks there's any risk of our doing that, but their lawyers said we must be the ones to make the decision on the Retirement Fund. My memo follows:

1. A price of nine times earnings is not ridiculously high for the stock. Retton has sold at this level before.
2. The management has been able to maintain its dividend for the last five years and has earnings to support it. The yield is better than the Dow Jones 30-stock average.
3. Motley says it will close down certain unprofitable Retton operations when it gets control. That is certainly believable in light of its past procedures on increasing the earnings of acquired companies. One recently unprofitable Retton operation has been the dumbbell plant by the train station. We have an already high unemployment rate in this city,

and a loss of jobs would put a financial burden on the state and the city as well as cause social dislocation.

4. We would not want to own Motley stock. It is the kind of operation that is very hard to anticipate. Looking back you can see why Motley stock sold at a price earnings multiple higher than the market, but I would not be comfortable predicting future earnings or stock prices. So if we tendered and the tender were successful, we would want to sell the Motley stock. On the other hand, if we did not tender and they won, our accounts would end up in a minority position. Under these circumstances, our stock might not bring the $42 a share it was selling for last year: there is no reason to assume that Motley would extend its tender offer once it had achieved control.

5. Theoretically, if we were convinced Motley was going to lose we could sell the stock now at $58 and then buy it back at, maybe, $40 after Motley has lost. But that's a short-term operation and even if Motley lost we'd have to be very skillful and very right. We are not speculators. There is a risk, too, that the sale would put a block in the hands of Motley, thus helping them win. The penalties for being wrong would be severe in terms of our image, not just with Retton and the local employees but with other customers. More than image, our reliability. Even if we sold and bought back Retton shares and Motley lost, Retton would be very upset with what would look like our walking out on their interests. And justifiably so!

Has MacReed approached this problem in a way that adds an ethical dimension? She appears to have identified the major issues confronting her as an analyst and portfolio manager. It is, however, equally possible that the memorandum is a whitewash for a decision already taken in accordance with the expectations of the Retton management that the 10 and 7 percent blocks represent a secure vote for management. Motive—state of mind—is relevant in ethics. So we need to examine her personal integrity. MacReed is at least addressing the idea of selling into the market in order to pick up sixteen points. That is an imaginative, albeit unlikely, contribution to the current controversy. The overall impression is that as a professional she is trying to identify alternatives, however improbable, while at the same time recognizing that the mainstream answer is to stay with Retton management.

Her list is not simple brainstorming but shows her consciousness of probable consequences. She begins with her technical responsibility for investments, analyzing the reasonableness of the offered price, although her analysis is somewhat superficial at first glance and perhaps even contrived. Then she shifts to the impact of a takeover, identifying who could be adversely affected: the local community, local Retton employees, and, by inference, her firm. She touches on the adverse consequences to the investment if the takeover is rejected, but also recognizes that this holding is not simply a piece of paper: it is an investment in a real entity, as a theatre "company" is more than the producer's money, but involves individual actors, directors, and backstage employees.

It is uncomfortable for both parties to question whether an analysis is made in good faith. Certainly it would be unrealistic for a person in MacReed's position to ignore the probable outcome of the analysis, which will be to support Retton and continue with the investment. But if the analysis is simply documentation that was supplied to support a prefabricated conclusion, we are being manipulated. This was explored with MacReed, who developed the following points.

I can understand your raising the question. It is hardly flattering but I won't take it personally. It is easy to get carried away supporting the people who are "on your side." I like the people at Retton. I think they're doing a good job. And I want to see them continue. On the other hand, I live with change in financial and business affairs. One thing that I learned after I got out of school is that if you project tomorrow from yesterday you're going to be burned. So I do try to anticipate what might occur regardless of whether I like it or not.

Maybe I outlined Motley's offer too quickly during our conversation. I assumed you had the details and would know that I have them, but let me clarify this for you. Motley is in numerous businesses. In the last four or five years they must have acquired half-a-dozen companies in different businesses from eye drops to mortgages. The tactic was generally to negotiate the acquisitions, after taking an investment position and pushing the target management into a corner. Their standard operating procedure is to buy just under 10 percent of the company, hold it for a while, and then begin to flex their muscles. That's sort of what has happened here. Motley's assault started off with an acquisition of less than 5 percent of Retton's common stock. We now know that they bought pretty steadily for a couple of months, acquiring 4.9 percent and stayed there. There was no blip in the stock price or special increase in volume of trades—no rumors or communication. So Retton did not know that anything was up.

While Retton's cash position has been very good, the management team has not paid a lot of attention to the possibility that Retton might someday be a target. They, themselves, have not engaged in acquisitions and their legal department is mainly concerned with leases and labor relations. They are not really tuned to the corporate battle scenario.

Anyway, to get back to Motley, four months passed, there was a drop in Retton's reported earnings, no special new products, pricing was rigid, and costs escalated. The price of the stock dropped a couple of points and Motley bought up all the stock they could find in a week. They did not have to file with the S.E.C. until ten days after exceeding 5 percent, so Retton was still in the dark until they learned Motley owned 9 percent. (Certain things happen at 10 percent that are not necessarily what a raider would like. Specifically, an antitrust filing is required and any profit on Retton shares has to be disgorged when the time between the purchase and sale or sale and purchase is less than six months.)

At 9 percent Motley announced the tender offer. It is my understanding that they called the president of Retton to say this was going to happen. I think it was a Friday when the call came and the tender was to be public the following Monday. I guess the tone was superficially friendly, but who was kidding whom? In any event, the tender offer was then spelled out for 41 percent more of Retton stock at the price of $63, as you know: one Motley share for one Retton share. Nothing for those who didn't tender.

Sixty-three dollars is a good price. When Retton sold at nine times earnings a number of years ago, sports stores were really just taking off. You could make a good case for a big expansion in basic items like soccer pads and basketball uniforms.

There are stockholder advantages to selling off some of the unprofitable businesses. Even the dumbbell plant is unpredictable and not important to the rest of the business, although it is an integrated operation that could be sold by Retton to its employees under certain reasonable financing agreements. Probably with increased employee incentives it could provide a living for its workers and not be a drain on Retton as far as future earnings growth is concerned. Sale of the plant would also provide added capital over time that could be used to develop some of their retail stores. But I certainly can't see that sort of employee stock ownership deal being worked out by Motley. They would just close the plant down and sell off half the company at knock-down auction rates in order to end up with a few small divisions that happen to adhere to some grand design of Motley's. What a waste. It would have been just a fancy exercise in arithmetic, affect the pension beneficiaries in unknown ways, create job losses for current wage earners, change expectations for people of our city, discourage a group of people who have worked well together for several years, and break up a team that has produced a product in which customers can have confidence. All this just doesn't make sense. It's not as though we bought the 10 percent of Retton stock to protect management. It's been in the fund for years.

The Greatest Good for the Greatest Number

MacReed's effort to be open-minded and test the consequences of her decisions reflects the attitude of the ethical utilitarian to identify the effect of actions, inactions, and decisions. She recognizes the difference between the vested pension beneficiaries and that of current workers, especially since it is possible that the merger could provide larger benefits and greater retirement security to vested beneficiaries than would be achieved through resisting the tender offer. She has also identified Retton's geographical community as a constituency.

MacReed has not answered clearly the need to assess priorities: who comes first and to what extent is each harmed or benefitted? Is her firm's sole contractual duty to protect the pensions of the vested beneficiaries because the firm is a sort of a trustee? That seems overly legalistic. As we have seen repeatedly, our relations to others don't stay in neat compartments. The beneficiaries live in a community with ties to Retton, some are currently employed by Retton. There is a seamless web of real-life contracts. She must properly look further than a trustee/beneficiary circle. The major pension fund beneficiaries may well be the higher-paid individuals. But the likelihood of harm on an individual basis is often harshest for employees who lack the resources to deal with a loss of benefits.

The wise professional must take into account both the people affected by the decision and the significance the benefit or dislocation has for them. Both must be analyzed when reviewing the relationship between the affected person and the decision maker. The dislocation of greatest consequence, here too, may be felt by the lower-paid employees, who may lose their jobs, and by the community, which will suffer from the domino effect of increased unemployment. The greatest benefits could be the opportunity for Retton shareholders to earn $58 a share in the current market and for retired employees to enjoy potentially greater security. MacReed's contractual obligation to the pension trust, narrowly read, is only to those shareholders who are vested beneficiaries. MacReed sees them as members of a community whose welfare is linked and must be considered as part of the greatest good for the greatest number.

More precise analysis of the potential effect an acquisition could have on the community is desirable if the community is to be treated fairly. If concerns of the city are to override the demonstrable benefit to pensioners of selling their shares at $58, these concerns must be very significant. How many jobs would be lost? How mobile are those people? Are there alternative sources of employment so that the length of unemployment for those who lose their jobs would be short? How likely are these assumptions? Are retraining options readily available to help ameliorate the negative effect? Is the dumbbell plant the only one at risk, and is a spin-off to the employees a realistic possibility? Is it probable that Retton, responding to its own need to remain viable, would also be likely to close down some or all of the plants in question? Is it an open-and-shut case that the shareholders would in the long run lose all opportunity for appreciation, or is there a possibility that $58 a share would be realized over a period of time whether or not Motley is successful? If the company is worth $63 to Motley, is there $63 of value if Retton pulls up its socks? If MacReed's decision is to hold the shares in perpetuity, will the probable flow of dividends and growth of capital compare favorably over time with other alternatives?

Deciding in Light of Future Decisions

How the firm acts here can establish a precedent for how the firm will behave in future similar situations. Central to sophisticated pragmatic partisans is consciousness of the future. A specific decision is rarely a precise rule for the future, but the methodology used to arrive at the decision is, for better or for worse, a definite precedent for formulating future decisions. Though unintended and often disregarded, all actions quietly develop precedents for the future. The process MacReed used to work through the problem facing Retton, and in turn the investment manager, will be consonant with the process used to find the correct solution for the next problem that arises. However practical, a decision reached inarticulately or insensitively sets a bad precedent for the future since there is no record of the process used to reach the decision. Some help can be gleaned from the process of the "common law," which is in essence an accumulation of precedents that are to be applied to new situations. The conduct of trustees is rooted in the need to resolve conflicting interests objectively, in an ethical manner. Fiduciary law, in turn, offers guideposts for many nontrustee relationships. We need all the help we can get: intuition, our best judgment, and the process of systematic reasoning. It is risky to rely on our first reaction, but we should not write off this reaction, especially since it can be (as Evelyn Waugh in *Brideshead Revisited* termed it) the "batsqueak" of apprehension, providing insight that straightforward reasoning will miss.

MacReed could explore selling the pension fund holding to Retton at, say, $58 a share, the current market price, or perhaps work out a put option at a lesser figure, preserving the opportunity that may result from the merger threat. Should she go beyond the intuition that the longtime holding of the 10 percent Retton position is to be continued and seek outside advice from the participants in the plan as to their desires? Or from a professional consultant? In pursuing even these participatory devices she must recognize that either or both can be misused, manipulated to ratify a desired decision, and cause stress and loss of control instead of increasing openness and decentralizing the process.

New situations can be envisioned to test the decision as a precedent. For example, how would MacReed handle the Retton stock if Motley were also a major customer? If the community and the trusts are the objects of her affection there should be no change in the process of analysis and reasoning. What if Retton were to announce that it would close down unprofitable plants, including the local dumbbell factory, whereas Motley said it intends to keep them open? Such questions get at whether the negative effect on the local community as a concerned group is real or an advocate's argument.

It is only human for MacReed to conclude that the "home team" is the good guy and the "visiting team" is the adversary. If Retton ultimately decides to close the dumbbell plant and Motley wishes to expand the plant because it complements certain already profitable operations, it is harder for MacReed to know whom to cheer for. That is all the more reason to utilize a systematic approach when analyzing the situation, first considering the best interests of those who rely on her, in this case the pension beneficiaries, and then raising suspicions about any conclusion that supports her career.

The rights of affected groups and the responsibilities of a judicious decision maker occupy different sides of the same coin. Each provides a valid starting point for an analysis to complement and refine pragmatic insights. MacReed might tighten her analysis by examining the effect on the interested persons in two lights: is she acting in a manner that matches her inner compass of fairness? What would it be like if she were in their shoes? Are the other managed accounts that hold Retton stock apt to be enthusiastic about passing by the $63 share opportunity even if the Retton employees are?

How significant to the beneficiaries of the trust is this issue? How does the Retton pension trust work? Does the retirement plan pay *defined benefits* to the specific employee based on a formula related to the length of service and level of compensation? Pension fund assets collateralize the company's obligation, operating as a pledge of the assets needed to meet the obligation; they are held in custody by a bank and are managed by an outsider (MacReed) to assure the promised benefits. The retirement payment remains an obligation of the company, so that if the pension fund disappeared the employees would have to rely on the company's assets; if on the other hand Retton failed, the fund itself could become the sole source for such payments. Retton has a continuing tax incentive to make tax deductible distributions from its current income to the fund. There is legal pressure to achieve complete funding of benefits actuarially computed. There is management incentive to know that operating assets are not vulnerable to claims from unpaid employees. Is MacReed more comfortable passing the $63 tender opportunity because the retirement benefits are to be met by Retton as well as the pension fund? Each question begs further questions. Is the plan adequately funded to cover payments? If Motley's assault is repulsed at great cost, what risk is there to the viability of Retton? If the plan is overfunded, does the surplus belong to Retton rather than the employees? If Retton is financially shaky, a proper objective of the pension fund may be to try to stabilize Retton, keeping it viable. However, for the other customers holding Retton stock the shakiness urges a "sell" conclusion.

A *defined contribution* retirement plan operates differently. There Retton's payment obligation ends at the time of the contribution. Once the contribution is in the hands of the trustees the benefits to the employee depend on how well the portfolio is managed. Can MacReed properly look beyond the financial well-being of the beneficiaries of such trusts that hold Retton stock? Although the retired beneficiaries have a modest sales opportunity and are in a dependency relationship to MacReed, the dumbbell company employees, who are not so clearly associated with MacReed, may face substantial harm—the loss of their jobs. Does the level of harm or the degree of reliance determine who is our "neighbor?" How far do we reach? According to the nursery rhyme, "for want of a nail a war was lost," but in any event MacReed's obligation does not extend to protecting the Treasury of the United States by seeing that taxes are maximized! Nor does it extend to the effect on the psychological well-being of the president of Motley for gaining or losing the current takeover battle.

The eminent scholar Chief Judge Benjamin Cardozo analyzed the limits of legal responsibility in a classic opinion for the New York Court of Appeals:

> Plaintiff was standing on a platform of defendant's railroad after buying a ticket to go to Rockaway Beach. A train stopped at the station, bound for another place. Two men ran forward to catch it. One of the men reached the platform of the car without a mishap, though the train was already moving. The other man, carrying a package, jumped aboard the car, but seemed unsteady, as if about to fall. The guard on the car who had held the door open reached forward to help him in, and another guard on the train platform pushed him from behind. In this act the package was dislodged, and fell upon the rails. It was a package of small size, about fifteen inches long and was covered by newspaper. In fact it contained fireworks, but there was nothing in its appearance to give notice of its contents. The fireworks, when they fell, exploded. The shock of the explosion threw down some scales at the other end of the platform, many feet away. The scales struck the plaintiff causing injuries for which she sues.[VII-1]

In the decision, the court assumed that a guard caused the fireworks to be dislodged by his carelessness so that if the newspaper had contained a Tiffany glass pitcher that smashed when it fell the railroad would have had to replace the pitcher. Now the court asked who was legally responsible for the injury the scales caused the plaintiff, Mrs. Palsgraf. By analogy, if a robber points a gun at a victim and the gun accidentally goes off, killing the victim, the charge will be murder. The same result would seem to occur if it were a bystander who were killed. Should that line of thinking cover Mrs. Palsgraf's injury from the scales? Cardozo said that "if no hazard was apparent to the eye of ordinary vigilance, an act innocent and harmless, at least to outward seeming, with reference to her, did not take to itself the quality of a tort because it happened to be a wrong with reference to someone else." He continued:

> One who jostles one's neighbor in a crowd does not invade the rights of others standing at the outer fringe when the unintended contact casts a bomb upon the crowd. The wrongdoer is the man who carries the bomb, not the one who explodes it without suspicion of the danger. Life will have to be made over, and human nature transformed, before prevision so extravagant can be accepted as the norm of conduct. We are told that one who drives at reckless speed through a crowded city street is guilty of a

negligent act and, therefore, of a wrongful one in the sense that it is unsocial, but wrongful and unsocial in relation to other travelers only because the eye of vigilance perceives the risk of damage. If the same act were to be committed on a speedway or a race course, it would lose its wrongful quality.

In the same case Judge Andrews took a different approach in a dissenting opinion:

In an empty world negligence would not exist. It does involve a relationship between man and his fellows. But not merely a relationship between him and those whom he might reasonably expect his act would injure. Rather, a relationship between him and those whom he does in fact injure. If his act has a tendency to harm someone, it harms him a mile away as surely as it does on the scene. The proposition is this: everyone owes to the world at large the duty of refraining from those acts that may unreasonably threaten the safety of others. Such an act occurs. Not only is he wronged to whom harm might reasonably be expected to result, but he also who is in fact injured, even if he be outside what would generally be thought the danger zone. There needs be duty due the one complaining, but this is not a duty to a particular individual because as to him harm might be expected. Harm to someone being the natural result of the act, not only that one alone, but all those in fact injured may complain.

We build a dam, but are negligent as to its foundation. Breaking, it injures property downstream. We are not liable if all this happened because of some reason other than the insecure foundation. But when injuries do result from an unlawful act we are liable for the consequences. It does not matter that they are unusual, unexpected, unforeseen, and unforeseeable. But there is one limitation. The damages must be so connected with the negligence that the latter may be said to be the proximate cause of the former.

Any philosophic doctrine of causation does not help us. A boy throws a stone into a pond. The ripples spread. The water level rises. The history of that pond is altered also. Yet it will be forever the resultant of all causes combined. Each one will have an influence. How great only omniscience can say. You may speak of a chain, or if you please, a net. An analogy is of little aid. Each cause brings about future events. Without each the future would not be the same. Each is proximate in the sense it is essential. But that is not what we mean by the word. Nor on the other hand do we mean sole cause. There is no such thing.

Should an analogy be thought helpful, however, I prefer that of a stream. The spring, starting on its journey, is joined by tributary after tributary. No man can say whence any drop of water is derived. Yet for a time distinction may be possible. Into the clear creek, brown swamp water flows from the left. Later, from the right comes water stained by its clay bed. The three may remain, for a space, sharply divided. But at last, inevitably no trace of separation remains. They are so commingled that all distinction is lost. As we have said, we cannot trace the effect of an act to the end, if end there is. Again, however, we may trace it part of the way. Murder at Sarajevo may be the necessary antecedent to an assassination in London twenty years hence. An overturned lantern may burn all Chicago. We may follow the fire from the shed to the last building. We likely say the fire started by the lantern caused its destruction.

A cause, but not the proximate cause. What we do mean by the word "proximately" is that because of convenience, of public policy, of a rough sense of justice, the law arbitrarily declines to trace a series of events beyond a certain point. This is not logic. It is practical politics. Take the illustration given in an unpublished manuscript by a distinguished and helpful writer on the law of torts. A chauffeur negligently collides with another car that is filled with dynamite, although he could not know it. An explosion follows. (A) walking on the sidewalk nearby, is killed, (B) sitting in a window of a building opposite, is cut by flying glass, (C) likewise, sitting in a window a block away, is similarly injured. And a further illustration. A nursemaid, ten blocks away, startled by the noise, involuntarily drops the baby from her arms to the walk. It is all a question of expediency.

There are no fixed rules to govern our judgment. There are simply matters of which we may take account.

In a different case, with complicated coincidental facts, Judge Friendly of the U.S. Court of Appeals said:

> We see no reason why an actor engaging in conduct which entails a large risk of small damage and a small risk of other and greater damage, of the same general sort, from the same forces, and to the same class of persons, should be relieved of responsibility for the latter simply because the chance of its occurrence, if viewed alone, may not have been large enough to require the exercise of care.

Somewhere a point will be reached where courts will agree that the link has become too tenuous—that what is claimed to be of consequence is only fortuity.[VII-2]

These discussions involve three ethical pragmatists and their efforts to draw a line of legal liability in a complex situation. Such efforts suggest how appealing it could be to MacReed to shift the Motley tender/hold decision from her shoulders to the owners. However, that is not without its own problems. Some problems are mechanical; others are philosophical, such as encouraging participation by an employee who lacks information and experience when such participation will be to that person's disadvantage. Peer pressure can virtually guarantee certain decisions to retain Retton stock.

The federal pension act—the Employee's Retirement Income Security Act (ERISA)—adds another layer, for it is founded on a dominant ethical commitment: moneys should be provided to a beneficiary on retirement. This policy is jeopardized if responsibility for the fund is transferred to uninformed people. Paternalism may be mandated by public policy.

The time limits on the Motley offer make a shift of the decison on the Retton holdings almost certainly unfeasible in any event. So the decision remains: the fiduciary retains a pastoral responsibility to protect each fund, and the personal integrity of MacReed as the manager becomes the fulcrum of a fair decision. The special risk, even in this situation where a strong, experienced, sensitive manager is at the controls, lies in our universal ability to delude ourselves. Self-deception is unlimited. Or more accurately, as Stanley Hauerwas points out, "the irony of self-deception is that a cynic is less vulnerable to self-deception than a conscientious person."[VII-3] Stressing the tragic element of harm that results despite the best of efforts, Hauerwas addresses the conflict between our view of ourselves, our values, and our capacity, nothing that the extent of deception is directly related to "the type of story we hold about how and what we are."

If it is to counter our propensity to self-deception, the story that sustains our life must give us the ability to spell out in advance the limits of the various roles we will undertake in our lives. The story must enable us to discriminate within those roles the behavior that can easily entrap and blind us. The more noble and caring the role, the more discriminating the story must be. To lack such a story is to be deprived of the skills necessary to recognize or challenge the demonic. And to be bereft of those skills is to fall prey to these powers. That much we can now say, after Auschwitz.

Chapter 8

Team Spirit in the Company
When is Loyalty a Disability?

Directors of corporations can get confused as to which constituency they represent when they make decisions. It is easy for them to fall into the trap of thinking of the Corporation as equivalent to the senior officers they see at board meetings. That can lead to unwise and shortsighted results.

In this scenario our corporate actors are DOS/X, Superior Systems, and Reliance Software. DOS/X is a publicly held company engaged in the production of software for data processing systems. As it was sustaining significant losses, a special meeting of the board was called to discuss the viability of the firm and a possible merger with Superior Systems, Inc. (SSI). DOS/X had service and distribution strengths; SSI, a new entry, was creating state-of-the-art products. Two of the senior people at SSI had left DOS/X to form SSI.

As protagonist we have an experienced management and securities analyst, who is an outside director and a member of the audit committee of DOS/X, George Grinnell. His comments on the other actors and the plot follow.

> We were all very nervous about our losses and the erosion of our capital base. Our stock was still selling at $9½ but would drop fast when the bad news came out. Charlie Carlton, president, had kept in touch with the guys who organized SSI and he reported that there was a chance of a deal with SSI to keep DOS/X going.

> SSI was a private company and not interested in public shareholders. That could have been worked out, preserving our listing on the Exchange while giving them control on some basis. But they just wanted the company. The deal provided that four officers of DOS/X, including Charlie, would receive two-year employment contracts with SSI at their current salary levels and the shareholders

of DOS/X would each receive $10 a share, making it a wholly owned subsidiary of SSI. I did some work and gave a formal opinion that $10 was a fair price for the DOS/X shares, and we announced the merger plan for the shareholders to approve.

Just before the shareholders' meeting, Reliance Software, a competitor of ours, with shares traded over-the-counter, made a cash tender offer for all the shares of DOS/X at $12½. The offer was contingent on the rejection of the proposed merger between DOS/X and SSI. We adjourned the shareholders' meeting for a couple of weeks and then again for a month in order to discuss all this with SSI. Charlie came back to the board with a new deal he had been able to work out under which SSI would pay $14 a share.

To nail it down we agreed to give SSI a one-year irrevocable option to buy enough unissued shares at $14 a share to equal 200 percent of our current capital. That meant they would be sure to have the two-thirds vote needed to approve the merger, no matter what stock went to Reliance. By exercising the option SSI would have the necessary two-thirds vote in its hands. We worked out a letter to the shareholders announcing the new agreement and told the shareholders not to tender to Reliance.

By that point it was very hard to focus on any other business except this battle. As you can guess, we spent a lot of time back and forth on the telephone, and there were some stories in the press and a lot of inquiries from brokers and shareholders. The transaction volume in the stock had really picked up and the speculators were in the picture, placing their casino bets on the outcome. At that point, Reliance increased its offer to $15½ a share on the condition that the DOS/X SSI option deal be terminated.

Well, you know the rest.

For the directors to gain a proper perspective and for the DOS/ X shareholders to be able to cope with the situation it needs to be untangled. Let's review the central facts:

1. DOS/X was in financial trouble.
2. The officers could get employment contracts with a viable competitor, SSI, if they sold out DOS/X at $10 a share.
3. Grinnell, as a member of the DOS/X team, provided a fair price appraisal at $10, which the shareholders would be expected to rely on.
4. The price was well below what could have been negotiated in the market, i.e. at least $15½. The spread between $10 with

Charlie and his friends being employed and $15½ without that is 5½.

5. When the outside interest became clear, DOS/X and SSI tried to tie their deal down by giving SSI control before the shareholders' meeting rather than looking for the highest sale price.

The process by which DOS/X management sold out, or tried to, was inadequate by any standards. The shareholders had a charter-required right of participation in the decision, but communication to (and from) the shareholders was short-circuited. If the board members had any belief that they were acting properly it was because they were transfixed by short-term horizons and "team spirit." Their "team" included the senior officers and probably DOS/X creditors. Conceivably, their finances were so meager that the creditors in effect already "owned" the company and were being treated as though they were the preferred shareholders. The members of the team who were left behind included the true shareholders. They have been treated as though they were unable to make a decision that would affect them, a decision that is being preempted by the board—which had access to all the facts and then gave priority to the quantifiable self-interest of the officers. No reference is made to investment bankers, who must have been interested in the situation in light of the two offers that came in; no distinction is made between those shareholders, whose financial incompetence requires reliance on outside experts such as the DOS/X board, and others who can fend for themselves if they have the information to which they are entitled; those who could fend for themselves received inadequate information. The passing reference to speculators is ripe with an indication of the larger world (a world treated as an enemy) that is gathering to watch or participate; the nonofficer employees' future under the deal with SSI is not mentioned. It is as though a transaction had been taking place in a dark corner of the city square at midnight when the klieg lights suddenly came on, casting a new light and creating new dimensions to the scene. Moving around the square in Breugelian complexity are shareholders of DOS/X, SSI, and Reliance; corporate managers; employees of both corporations; creditors, including personal and commercial bankers; customers and suppliers; auditors, lawyers, consultants on strategy, and public relations counsel; brokers, and investors.

Is this a question of 20/20 hindsight? Would there have been any ethical problem if Reliance had not made its offer? Yes, there almost certainly would have been. The process lacked analysis. The decision was to take the company private and cut off the future opportunity for the shareholders whom the board was supposedly representing, 69 and to do so without candor and without testing the best price. The manipulative pro forma $10 appraisal was a key element. Participation by the shareholders could be only minimal and based on a scintilla of information.

In previous chapters, three ethical philosophies have been discussed. There are, of course, others, and the DOS/X board may have had one of its own. If so, what was it? In his article, "Making Business Ethics Work,"[VIII-1] Henry B. Arthur lists ten ethical philosophies:

Hedonism—the self as number one; from narrowly conceived selfishness on to "sublimations" of the self

Utilitarianism—the greatest good for the greatest number

Pragmatism—whatever minimizes conflict; a 'workable' set of rules

Salvation—earning redemption via good works

Salvation—obtained through isolation, meditation, and individual devotion

Golden Rule—virtue based on faith and charity; Christian doctrine

Divine Right (of kings, etc.)—leadership hierarchies, each has his own place, comfort, or displeasure in a "pecking-order" society

Egalitarianism—push down the rich, push up the poor

Paternalism—protectivism; statism; security blanket; freedom from fear

Physiocrats—what is natural is good; nature is somehow sacred

The DOS/X board has perhaps used a combination of hedonism, divine right, and paternalism. Was that what the shareholders were led to expect?

When the issue came up, Grinnell began and ended with the price. He should have started with the "social contract" that management is to run the company under the informed guidance of the board for the benefit of the shareholders. This benchmark would have had very practical applications when he came to the pre-question of whether he could give an objective opinion on the fairness of the price, one on which the shareholders could properly rely.

At the first stage of the merger, the stock price may have seemed fair. The deal benefitted the shareholders by a slightly better than market price, and also benefitted the corporate management that Grinnell had been working with and which presumably chose him as director. It is true that the management promoted its self-interest by developing employment contracts with a viable entity, but this was disclosed to the shareholders and Grinnell may very well have acted in good faith, seeing this as a legitimate deal.

The ethical difficulty arose in the next stage when the facts changed dramatically. When a new contender added a 25 percent premium to the price, Grinnell and the board were obligated to rethink the situation. The actions of the new contender had proved Grinnell's conclusion wrong: this was not just a friendly and routine deal. He must have expected shareholders to rely on him. It was essential for him to start over and view the situation from the beginning— a task that is hard for anyone. Think of how often a person who buys a stock is apt to keep it when its price drops and its earnings come in lower than estimated. The tendency is to identify new reasons to justify holding the stock: the dividend as a percent of price has increased; since the stock is cheaper it is more attractive; a hope that the stock will do better in the long-term. It may be right to retain faith in the stock, but a new assessment is needed with a minimum of self-justification and as much of a fresh outlook at the situation as possible.

Instead of reevaluating the situation, however, when the situation changed, Grinnell marched forward with the pack to find a way to complete the original deal with a minimum of change. As a professional he should have discarded his earlier appraisal and prepared a new one. By producing another analysis he could investigate alternatives, demanding more details on the Reliance offer and its effect on the company. Rather, he helped develop a shield for the SSI deal with the option arrangement, so that no matter what the shareholders decided a price of $14 would be impregnable. Since there is no indication of any disunity among the members of the board, it would appear the decision was taken unanimously. Not only was Reliance being blocked, but so was any other bidder that might have paid a higher price.[VIII-2]

Loyalty

Loyalty is a wonderful ethical underpinning of society. In the DOS/X-Reliance case, Grinnell was loyal to the team composed of Charlie Carlton, the president, and the board. In turn, after its difficult financial problem was solved by the commitment of SSI, SSI became another partner in this enterprise and another to whom his loyalty was given. Loyalty to your cadre can be a trap; it can be the source of discrimination in employment, constipation in long-term planning, and lack of interest in bringing into a management group specialists with a command of the implications of details— "knowledge workers." Grinnell's need to extend his loyalty to the broader group of shareholders was forgotten. Whether loyalty should be extended beyond shareholders to include suppliers, customers, and the community at large was not addressed at all.

A Second Chance

Contemporary theatre permits alternate denouements selected by the audience. If the events of the DOS/X situation were repeated in a situation in which you were involved, how should you act in light of the experience you have gained from Grinnell? How would you handle your role as director? When would you begin to act differently from Grinnell? Wouldn't you choose to change the script before the very first negotiation? When you learn that the company is experiencing financial difficulties, shouldn't you compose a checklist of the considerations to be taken into account when formulating a solution? An analyst is added to a board because his or her skills and experience bring value and legitimacy to the management. The fact that the board expresses a need for your particular services is apt to be part of the reason why you joined the board. Once on the board you tend to be pleasant, to bend your views to meet those of the other members who have a broader knowledge of the company, its history, and its goals. That can be proper, but there is a "catch-22" in this situation: you are valuable to the board because of your skills and knowledge, yet you reduce your value when you dilute and suppress your perceptions to conform with others. As an analyst you are expected always to bring your special insights and experience to the issues at hand.

When it becomes clear that your company may not survive on its own, the analyst is pushed to the forefront. This gives you an opportunity, indeed a responsibility, to take command of the manner in which the issue at hand is analyzed. You are trained as a "numbers person" and are expected to quantify the issues. In taking command of the situation, return to the checklist you made at the first signs of trouble. Start using the list to put the issues and people affected by the company's troubles in some kind of order: creditors, customers, long-term suppliers, productivity, employees, officers, shareholders, product control. Then begin to draft a methodology for the board, a structure for analyzing developments deciding on an outline of who is to participate and what goals are to be achieved. Your training will serve as a constant light for the board during this murky period. Throughout the decision making process, you may be overruled and your best ideas may at times seem unimaginative and disappointing. But your efforts will ensure that the sole rallying point in the decision making process will not be a distorted "rah-rah" definition of loyalty to those you see most often.[VIII-3]

Chapter 9

Best Execution and the Super Bowl
Brokerage Policy and the Institutional Trader

Institutional investors execute a myriad of transactions in stocks, bonds, short-term paper, and other securities. The captain of the trading desk continually makes decisions that affect the investment results for the institution and its customers. While prices continually change, only recently have transaction costs changed; for most of its history, the New York Stock Exchange had fixed transaction commission rates. As comparable skill in the execution of transactions was widely available, friendship, golf, service, and research were the basis of selecting brokers to execute client transactions. The present day "wild card" of flexible and negotiable commissions was not available. Indeed, flexible commissions was expressly prohibited by the Codes of Ethics of the Exchanges, a prohibition supported by the government.

In 1975, the S.E.C. ceased to approve commission rates, leaving rates to be fixed by competitive forces. In selecting brokers for execution, institutional investors learned to add negotiation of commission levels to friendship and other traditional forms of supplementary service provided by brokers.[IX-1]

In a large institutional investor one professional may make the specific investment decision, another may implement that decision through execution, and a third may handle transaction settlement and recordkeeping. In a small firm one person may handle all phases. In either case there is an ethical responsibility to do the best for the client whose assets are being used to pay transaction costs.[IX-2]

The scene is laid at the the Mefford Trust Company, a trustee for many regional pension accounts. On stage is Martin Wittenberg, head trader. Other business colleagues and friends come and go. His comments follow.

I have been working at the bank's trading desk for ten years. Before that I worked for a retail broker—a wirehouse.

In the old days when commissions were fixed, the bank pretty much divided up our business among brokers with local offices, and they were all customers of ours. In 1975—"May Day" — fixed commissions were outlawed. The major firms in the business continued to provide us with good service and we stuck with them. We didn't get mixed up with fly-by-nighters who came in cutting prices and eliminating services.

We're always under pressure from the pension fund customers for good investment ideas, and we need all the stock research we can get. If we dealt with some no-name pipe rack firm in New York, we'd find we had no research. Finally, discounters like that don't position securities so that large block trades are out of the question with them.

The old-line firms around town are just the opposite: they give us all sorts of research help and they help us to get new issues of stocks that are rationed out because of high demand. There is nothing as maddening as knowing that a new stock is going to sell above the offering price because the issue is already presold and the unsatisfied demand will push the price up in the after-market. Small companies—high-tech, high-risk, Silicon Valley ventures—they don't fit in the customer portfolios. But it is great for the morale of the people in the bank to be allocated those stocks for their own accounts.

It's more than service that we get from the brokers. We also get a lot of business from them. Brokers' loans to their customers are an important revenue source for the brokers and, when we lend money to the broker, important to us, too. With long-distance discounters you don't see any of that. I don't mean we only pick the brokers who have loans with us. We are a very ethical group and go to block traders from time to time if there is a big block— big brokers like Goldman Sachs, and so on. As most of our activity is buying and selling in hundred-share lots spread over a period of time, we don't have to get into the block transactions much. We're long-term investors for our customers.

One of our major sources of information is Jerry Grottle who works for a firm in town that is a member of the National Association of Securities Dealers, the N.A.S.D. They deal in small companies, O.T.C.—over-the-counter stock market.

Jerry does a lot of local research. They generally make a market in the local stocks we deal with, so it's like calling directly to a floor broker on the stock exchange floor.

You have to know people personally to have a sense of their

reliability. That's important in making judgment calls. We know Jerry and his firm pretty well and see them after hours. They have box seats at the local proteam games and we have a rule that we rotate the seats and take a customer or prospect, not just a social binge with your wife or kid. Every year there's a chance to go to the Super Bowl for their best customers and you can be sure Mefford is at the top of that list. Usually the president of the bank goes and takes one of the directors.

Officers get commissions on new business we bring into the bank. In my position I've been able to introduce a lot of agency customers sent to me by our brokers. Every doctor within fifty miles has a broker and you find that they have pension plans where they need a bank to act as custodian and manager and to keep the records. There's loan business, as I mentioned, and some tax shelter opportunities at the end of the year. Well, as you work with the brokers and they become confident you're not going to take their customers away, they are happy to bring in more business. The more you work together the more you *can* work together.

I mentioned hot issues. Well, Jerry has been a lot of help. A lot of new companies in this part of the country come to market in the O.T.C. And I've built up a nice little portfolio over the years. Basically, I buy and hold. Over a period of time, several of these little companies have had mergers and ended up listed on the stock exchange. Every once in a while one of them fails, so you have to get a good assortment of them in order to make it work. Anyway, Jerry keeps me in mind and gives me a call when he sees something interesting coming along. There is no conflict with the pension funds because they don't buy high risk.

Our compliance department keeps us on our toes. There is a "Chinese wall" between the loan department and the traders, so we don't even know about new deals the bank is financing until they're up and running. You know, once I sold some stock I owned just before the bank sold a big block in a private deal and the price took a tumble. Well, the compliance guy was all over me. Had I heard there was a big sale coming? Why did I sell? All that. They really watch those' things.

There is no law against Martin Wittenberg being a personal investor: he picks the brokers but not the stock in which the clients are going to invest; he doesn't have authority to churn the portfolio, since the frequency of transactions is determined in another department. Wittenberg's problem is that he doesn't understand that his customers' buying power, not his, brings into his own portfolio new issues with a level of demand that assures a higher price in the aftermarket. Perhaps his actions are not surprising when we consider that the management of Mefford Trust seems to miss this point: the personal tickets for the Super Bowl Game that are offered by the brokers are paid for by the transactions of Mefford's customers. Wining and dining a director on the broker's dollar is discomforting. It is more than a *quid pro quo* for past brokerage business; it is pressuring the bank to continue using that broker. It is also an incentive to churn the accounts and generate more commissions. This is a problem at Wittenberg's level, as well as at a more senior level. Indeed, in light of prospective loan business, the bank could justify paying the broker for its officer's tickets. Certainly the pro-game tickets should not be bought by their trust customers' dollars.

This type of back-scratching has brought business to the bank and to Wittenberg himself, due in part to lack of ethical guidance from the bank. The distinction between benefits to the bank and costs to the customers must be addressed at the highest level. Who pays? Who receives the benefits? These questions should have a common answer. It is hard to believe a brokerage firm is charging the lowest price for services (the negotiated commission if it is acting as a broker/agent; the spread between bid and asked prices if it is acting as principal/dealer)—someone has to pay for the entertainment and other perks. Transactions in the over-the-counter market, where price and commission are bundled together, can be particularly vulnerable to this type of exploitation.

Traditionally, receiving research materials from brokers in return for customer brokerage has not involved the same ethical problems as long as execution skills and commissions are competitive, and research is the object rather than a cosmetic to cover the real intent of obtaining new business or tickets to the Super Bowl. Generating research is part of the broker's regular business; it benefits the customer.

The Mefford pattern involves an entire series of potential problems: higher turnover generates more commissions and congenial negotiations on commissions generate more profits for the broker. In turn, Jerry Grottle has his entertainment budget![IX-3]

Reformation

By accepting tickets to the Super Bowl, Mefford's president encourages others in the bank to participate in such practices. Sad to say, Wittenberg may be carrying out precisely the job for which he is paid: generating perks for top management as well as himself. If so, he will be in a very awkward situation when he realizes his wrongdoing and wants to correct it. To whom can he complain when he realizes the bank is exploiting customers? How could he complain to the president, who encourages such exploitation? As a way of refocusing attention, some legal concerns might be expressed. If he were to cast himself as a somewhat bumbling, straightforward, and loyal employee he could, after a little research, come to the compliance department with a story along these lines:

The other night after work I had a drink with some of our broker friends as I often do. They were complaining about the other banks in town tightening up on commissions and trades. Jerry Grottle was fit to be tied, as you can imagine. There is some software program the banks have that collates the cents per share on each transaction into a report and ignores the way we have always done it—just showing total dollars, or sometimes the discount from the 1975 Stock Exchange Commission Schedule, like "40 percent off." Of course, we show nothing except price on new issues or trades in the over-the-counter market. That has always been fine for us and the customers have never asked for anything else as far as I know.

One of these guys mentioned that a lawsuit has been brought against a big bank in New York for choosing the brokers who are their own loan customers. And then another guy said that there was even a problem about brokers getting commission business from mutual funds they bring customers to. I don't know what it was all about. The guys were getting very upset. One of them even said he had heard some investment firms make you clear all your personal trades before you make them. We've been pretty liberal on all that and as far as I can see it has never hurt our customers. We have a lot of very good people working for our bank and if they take a step you can be pretty sure that it's all right. But with all of that talk I got a little upset about whether there might be criticism of the bank and whether I should do something about guidelines.

That certainly might get some action without Wittenberg being blamed for not being a team player.

Professional fiduciaries are likely to have discretion over the selection of the broker executing transactions. This is also true of an in-house pension committee running a retirement benefit fund and of institutional intermediaries such as investment managers, insurance companies, or trust companies. In the bond market, choosing a broker is essential to the effectiveness of a transaction: the specific security selected will depend on availability and price at that moment. By way of contrast, listed stocks can often be placed with any of several brokers who offer good competitive executions. This reflects not only the high level of competence of many brokerage firms, but also the massive volume and high-quality mechanics of exchange markets; however, large transactions can result in different prices depending on the selection of the broker. This leads to the basic rule that many fiduciaries adopt for the selection of brokers: the "best"—or more accurately "competitive"—execution possibilities for the particular transactions must be available from the broker selected to complete that transaction. In other words, choose the broker with the extra research "unless better elsewhere."

When selecting a broker for a customer, we must consider what the price and the transaction costs of execution will be and whether the broker will provide prompt settlement and satisfactory delivery. In making the selection one must work from a list of firms capable of providing satisfactory execution on the transaction in question and must affirm that the commission and any other execution-related costs are competitive with others.

Wittenberg has shown that there are real conflicts of interest between the broker/dealer and the investor, and between the investor and the investor's representative who selects the broker. Hockey tickets, a credit line on someone else's American Express Card, business possibilities, and personal investment opportunities are temptations that can smack of fraud on the customer.

Investment research differs, as it can be a fringe benefit that aids the customer. From an ethical point of view, since research is closely tied to client results, it is a proper item to take into account in the selection between otherwise competitive brokers. For instance, suppose that a hundred shares of General Motors stock is being sold and that GM is the kind of stock sold by most brokers with equal effectiveness. No block transaction is being put together by Mefford Trust and brokers X, Y, Z will execute the transaction at the same price and at $0.10 a share. The code of ethics of the intermediary prohibits acceptance of hockey tickets or other gifts and favors, including new business introductions, as criteria for selection of brokers for client transaction. In the past, investment research offered by a firm we can call Mainstream Brokers has been useful to the customers. Under the circumstances, Mainstream is selected.

Even in such a case there can be conflicts. If Mainstream had signed a contract to provide research to Mefford Trust for a specific total "soft dollars" of commissions from customer accounts, there are two potential distortions in the process of selection: pressure on customers' accounts to generate the specific dollar amount of brokerage apart from investment needs, and pressure to choose Mainstream. The question that has to be asked each time is "is this transaction occurring to generate the agreed on dollars or is it for investment needs?" If last year's commissions for bank customers totalled a million dollars and the firm made a million dollar commitment to brokers for research for this year, the pressures would be enormous and obvious. If the commitments only totalled $10,000 the pressure would be minimal.

A similar dilemma arises for the institutional intermediary if the research is also available for cash, as well as soft dollars. In all reality, it is unlikely that the commission rate is competitive if the broker is offering a free bonus of a costly product for which others pay significant "hard dollars" of their own. Examples of such expensive research might be institutional performance analyses; pension fund liability and asset allocation studies; portfolio characteristics models offered in printed form or through software programs and tapes. Otherwise the broker will be in the poorhouse. So, the institution could wisely install a special internal approval system to take a fresh look at each case where there is a hard dollar alternative.[IX-3] A practical, publicized, and enforced code of ethics is essential.

Chapter 10

Ethics on the Buy Side
Thinking of the Investor

Putting the client's interest first requires a great deal of specific knowledge about how transactions work. Without a grasp of such details the alternatives cannot be identified, let alone measured properly against each other. While principles of self-interest and looking-out-for-the-other-person don't change, the details are constantly changing, especially at the margin. As a result, ethics must come from the managers who process transactions rather than an ethicist who is briefed on the case.

We need to look at an investment management firm affiliated with mutual funds and a trust company. Its investment management is primarily for pension funds and has traditionally relied on research provided by stockbrokers. The firm has been troubled by the recent increase of a practice where pension funds direct that a percentage of brokerage is to go to a specific brokerage firm in return for services, products, or cash provided to the fund, thus bypassing their manager. On stage is a senior executive, Spenser Bamford.

Our policy requires us to allocate brokerage only to a firm that can offer competitive price, execution, and commission for the transaction. The commission on the particular transaction is important, but you must also measure factors such as the depth and quality of service at the execution level. As between brokers who are equally competitive, we choose those who provide helpful research to us.

Research from brokerage firms started as a way to reuse the materials their people prepared for the investment banking departments. The firms condensed information for the retail customers and presented it differently with more detail for institutions like us. Now, a lot of that good solid analysis is being risked by the use of "converter firms"—brokerage firms that have no independent research but in return for basic brokerage will supply products directly to customers, bypassing managers like us. That reduces our pool of discretionary brokerage for obtaining research, and the research we now get may be cut in turn.

I can understand how attractive it may be for the members of a pension committee to spend five days at the Aspen Institute dealing with the great philosophers, or to save on office expenses such as the *Wall Street Journal,* a Prentice Hall tax service, a C.C.H. pension service, or a software accounting system—things that the plan now buys for cash. If customer-directed brokerage to the converters continues to expand, there is that much less brokerage available for brokers who do good, imaginative investment research work. That damages the health of established brokers offering a range of facilities, and hurts the pension fund in the end. The converter is just a catalogue house that provides bare bones brokerage service.

If the real brokers are undercut, there has to be a concern for the long-term viability of the markets. As you ratchet commissions down it will be harder and harder to arrange block transactions or other difficult executions. It is all very well to say that you will only give easy trades—"no-brainers"—to the converter and give difficult trades to established firms. That doesn't wash: taking the easy trades away from a top firm has a pricing effect on that firm as it previously took into account the commissions on no-brainers in setting commissions for difficult trades. Now it will have to charge more for tough trades. They will not have the flexibility to absorb mistakes that come along in the ordinary course of our business. There will be no margin for error in case we miscalculate, such as mistakenly selling an issue of a preferred the client didn't hold —where our sell ticket transposed a digit. And, of course, in the long run there can be general disaster. Street research and public information would dry up unless there are enough commission dollars for top brokers to pay top analysts.

Managing brokerage relations is very complicated. For example, we have management rules on personal securities transactions that are designed to keep us from "gun jumping." I can't invest for my personal account before the clients. To reduce speculation, and be less vulnerable to outside pressures, I can't have a margin account. We test employees for drugs, too. As a result, we really don't have any basis for selecting brokers except their performance.

A lot of pension funds have come to the conclusion that there are excess charges in the industry, and they should try to reduce their own administrative expenses by rebates of commissions. That's all very well, except it doesn't come free. The cost of diverting millions of dollars from research not only harms the broker with a big capital investment in institutional research, it affects the way we operate. Apart from the research, which in itself is useful to the customers, we get a lot of information about what other people are thinking and doing. There is no substitute for knowing that. Let's say you estimate that a company is going to earn $4 next year and everyone else is talking about $3; you have a real advantage as a buyer. But you are going to have to know whether the consensus is $3 or $5 to make a judgment. If the consensus is $5, maybe you should be a seller. If half your discretionary brokerage is taken away by customers directing it to converters who don't help in the investment decision, your ability to identify the consensus is that much harder.

I realize there are managers who use street research to save themselves the cost of hiring analysts. That is not our case, but even for the firms that are criticized for doing precisely that, the point is overstated. The manager still has to make the investment decision based on his or her own judgment rather than any single piece of information. There is an infinite amount of information out there, and no matter how much you get there is some Parkinson's Law that says you hunger for more. Research isn't just written reports. Most of the really good help comes from telephone discussions between our people and those on the Street, not hot tips but experts talking, back and forth, brainstorming about details, helping each other fill in the gaps.

We all question how much research we should actually "manufacture" ourselves and how much we should "buy." We have our own analysts, we pay cash for a lot of research, and we get a lot of commission-generated information. If commissions are squeezed to the point where brokers must give only a bare bones execution service, the public will have less public information, that will cause the markets to become less efficient and more volatile, and the practice of exchanging hot tips under the table will be more widespread. Over the long-term that kind of market is contrary to the interest of the pension fund sponsors and the pensioners.

The other day a deal came along allowing us to shift expenses now paid by our mutual funds in cash from their investment income. The broker will transfer 40 percent of the commissions received on the fund's transactions to reduce the custody fee charged by the bank custodian. The proposal came from a top broker. By reducing the fund's expenses the shareholder's income would increase. Brokerage costs will not be higher than usual. At least this is what we would try to do. It's a very imaginative plan and we are going to experiment. It is not without costs, however. If $200,000 from their pocket goes to pay custody fees, it is not available to pay brokers' analysts. If we had to replace that $200,000 effort ourselves, we would have to increase our fees. It would be a wash. Moreover, our in-house research can never give the identical information about what other people are in fact thinking and doing.

I don't see a way out of this problem yet. One of the largest of the converter firms has taken the position that it will not provide services to the pension fund itself. Only to managers. That is a plus. There is also pressure from the U.S. Labor Department, which oversees pension rules. They are saying investment managers like us have a potential liability if commission benefits paid to the pension fund are not for the benefit of the pension beneficiaries. At least, when you do the trades for the fund, Labor says you have to see that the service is directed to the pension fund rather than to the employer sponsor. How can we second-guess whether it does indeed benefit the beneficiaries? We can make a judgment about using a mutual fund's brokerage to reduce the fund's custody fee. We know the fund business and can make an informed recommendation to the directors on what the trade-offs are. But the pension fund infrastructure is a different story.

It all smacks of the "give-up" orgy of the 1960s. Then, fixed commissions were too high for volume trades. What happened is sort of what happened to the airlines: the airlines undercut their approved fee schedules by throwing in automobile rentals and hotels. Result: the government took away their ability to fix fee schedules.

In the sixties the brokers met the pressure of institutions for lower prices by splitting commissions four ways to Sunday: pretending the fixed minimum commission schedules were still binding but rebating nevertheless. The government took away the Exchange's right to fix commissions.

With competition, the average commission for institutions is now about 8¢ a share. Granted some are lower and some are higher, but at any time there is a sort of competitive range of commissions. That range is under further assault as brokers "give up" to an outside vendor part of the negotiated commission in cash. If half the commission can be used to buy *Wall Street Journals* and software for a pension fund, people say how about giving the cash to the pension fund instead. Some of that is being done. The example I mentioned of the payment of the custody fee for the mutual funds is in fact a cash payment. Why not do it directly: simply reduce the cost of the trade by the same number of dollars? The reduction could even be a little more, because if the extra bookkeeping, accounting, and payment don't have to be made some administrative cost is saved. We expect to see lower rates. But then you come back to the other point. If there are lower rates, there are going to be fewer dollars available to pay for any extras, whether they are traditional research or these new services that have grown up. You need to anticipate the effect on your own business and how you can continue to provide your own service.

Bamford's *tour de force* is sophisticated and careful. (One wishes Wittenberg had had similar corporate/personal values and management imagination.) As Bamford indicated, in the "old days" stock exchange commissions for transactions were fixed by S.E.C.-approved schedules similar to those of public utility. They did not even involve a volume discount until quite late in the game: institutional transactions incurred a multiple of commissions precisely equal to however many hundreds of shares were involved in the trade. As the market went up and the transactions in equities by institutions soared, the absolute number of dollars being paid to brokers soared as well. In response, some innovative brokerage firms differentiated themselves by offering large customers a bonus service consisting of very sophisticated institution-oriented research materials.

As research boutiques often lacked truly competitive execution ability, another broker was often needed to execute the more complex trades for which the boutique was deemed "introducing broker." That nomenclature permitted the introducing and executing brokers to split commissions without violating the New York Stock Exchange rule prohibiting customer rebates. That split, expanded, was called a "give-up" (by the executing broker to another broker) and became widely used. It had its own built-in flaws as there were no guidelines on the propriety of "give-ups" and ultimately many customers and investment manager intermediaries created their own introducing brokers, transforming the "give-up" into a cash rebate. Although the seed of the system's destruction grew rapidly, regulatory guidance in the area was slow in coming and unpublicized.

It took quite a while for regulators and legislators to realize that while commissions were fixed, fringe benefits being provided to many investment managers were in effect rebates. Some benefits had no purpose other than client help. But there was at least one real-life vendor with a product permitting an investment management firm at the time even to purchase its own office furniture with its customers' commissions. A more usual commission give-up rewarded brokers for new business introductions to the manager. Why not? As commission rates were fixed, the customer wasn't paying any extra! Any broker introducing an advisory client expected to continue as the broker for the customer it had introduced. The broker would be outraged if a manager diverted the brokerage commissions of a common customer. Yet, as the complexity of trades increased, introducing brokers received less than 100 percent of the trades on an introduced account as institutions had to go to market makers to work out the large trades. So, the "customer's broker" expected enough extra brokerage from the investment managers's other accounts to make up at least the 100 percent.

As commission "give-ups" became commonly accepted in the 1960s and 1970s, managers limited the number of execution brokers, but directed as much as 40 percent of each commission back to brokers who brought them clients. Sales of both load and no-load mutual fund shares by brokers were similarly recognized through "give-ups" of fund brokerage. The practice even extended to the use of Mutual Fund A's commissions to reward sales of shares of Mutual Fund B, which had a common investment manager. Managers who used fund brokerage to serve their private interests precipitated an industry-wide series of private shareholder litigations, brought by the so-called "plaintiff's bar" on behalf of the mutual funds and their shareholders. The goal of these litigations was to force managers to disgorge commissions "given-up" for any purpose other than recapture for the client.

Although direct (cash) rebates were barred by the Exchange's constitution, a give-up system was developed on the Philadelphia Exchange to produce "legal" *de facto* cash rebates. A nonbroker investment manager would create an affiliate, register it as a broker, and have it join the National Association of Security Dealers. This nominal broker would, by affiliating with the Philadelphia Exchange, automatically and routinely collect in cash the 40 percent "finders fee" on transactions executed on that Exchange. The broker affiliated with the investment manager would receive and retain the rebated commissions, and the manager would reduce the investment advisory fee charged by it to the fund dollar for dollar. This two-step dance was deemed not to be an illegal rebate as the broker and the manager were separate corporations![X-1]

In due course the S.E.C. outlawed "give-ups" and, under the leadership of Senator Harrison Williams (Dem., N.J.), Congress substantially abolished fixed commissions. The prohibition was effective on "May Day" (May 1, 1975). The brokerage community generally had an understandable reluctance to create a price war or unnecessarily cut profits. Even today, more than a decade later, we hear commissions described as being at a "40 percent discount," a discount relative to a commission schedule established by the New York Stock Exchange under quite different circumstances prior to "May Day." While 40 percent sounds like a big discount, it may mean a price of 25¢ a share against today's institutional range of 2¢ to 12¢. A lot has happened.

Despite the reduction in commissions to these levels, many firms have prospered and, as Bamford points out, some brokers see enough "fat" in the system to further cut commissions.[X-2]

The battle Bamford is fighting involves many ethics-related issues: the nature of commissions, services, and products; the source of direction for brokerage allocation; the nature of the benefit to be derived by the investment manager; the benefit to the customer from the service. Do commissions "belong" to the broker? "Yes," says Jack Bober, president of Autranet, a major converter. If so, what does that mean? The institution's dollars are paid to the broker for services and indeed belong to the broker. But in designating the broker and the services the institution is directing a transfer of the customer's assets and is a fiduciary.

Any ability to choose involves responsibility for the foreseeable consequences of the choice. Changing business environments can be confusing, but the ethical need to align the benefit to the person whose money is being used remains an ethical constant. At first blush, the institutional client's input into which broker is selected for its own transactions and for what combination of services appears to address that concern. For many years, institutional clients have directed transactions in order to compensate brokers who provide the institution with measurement services concerning their investment managers' performance. The manager could hardly object to being evaluated, or to the small diversion of brokerage for a product. However, as institutions have become more aggressive, they have identified more and more services useful to them. Indeed, it has been reported that some institutions no longer ask the manager what percentage of brokerage they can allocate without interfering with the manager's responsibilities. They simply tell their managers how much is left for them to allocate, probably assuming a free ride on the research generated by other institutional clients of the managers.[X-3]

If the manager is placing the orders and the pension fund client's selection of the executing broker prevents competitive execution, the beneficiaries are at risk with a lot more to lose on the price of the trade than the value of some soft-dollar benefit. The manager is on the spot, can see what is happening, and has a continued obligation to speak up if the beneficiaries will not receive a fair deal. Beyond providing the best execution, a person on the spot needs to assess in an unbiased way the client benefit from all the soft-dollar products received.

Let's say Bamford decides to protect the interest of his beneficiaries, even at the cost of tangling with prospective pension plans that may not hire him. This concern jibes with his self-interest in getting "free" research of course, and he seems insensitive to two ethical issues (using client commissions to pay for manager errors and interfering with the privacy of employees through drug testing). But the analysis of commission diversion is supported by knowledge of the problem and of alternative specific tools. His concern and sophistication are indications of how complex applied ethics can be: unless you know the mechanics of the action you may not perceive the ethical problem or be able to justify its solution. The memo he issued to his order room and sent to all customers reads:

Client-Directed Brokerage and Soft Dollars

As manager we should accept client requests but not direction as to the broker we use. Only in this way will it be possible to achieve best execution.

We should not enter binding contracts with brokers with respect to the dollars of commissions accounts will generate, unless it is for a very small amount. Otherwise there is potential pressure to churn the portfolio and generate the necessary commission dollars needed to pay for the service, whether or not this is in the client's interest.

The soft-dollar benefit from client-directed brokers must be in the form of information related to investment decisions such as research reports, reports on economic trends, portfolio strategy analyses, performance measurement, or the like. Otherwise our clients must place their orders directly.

Any changes require case-by-case approval by me or my designee.

(This sort of instruction could have constructively changed Martin Wittenberg's life!)

Bamford's procedure to approve exceptions need not lead to bureaucratic horrors. Quick tests of the self-interest of the manager and the employer/sponsor of the retirement fund can be developed and routinized. For example, as computer software (and telephone line) products have become common, we need to ask which of these are properly the manager's contractual administrative expenses and whether there is a mechanism under which the manager can pay. An extreme example is magazine subscriptions, commercially available to the general public, which are supplied by the broker to the manager in return for commissions. In such an arrangement the manager's overhead is shifted to an uncomplaining customer who will never know what went on. Disclosure to the customer, even specific consent by the customer, would not be fair unless the customer understands the issue. Even if no shifting of overhead occurs, there is a need for sensitivity as the manager will weigh a product available for soft dollars differently than one paid in personal out-of-pocket cash. "Soft" dollars *are* dollars, however, being paid by the client; that tney are paid in the form of fees for bundled brokerage services makes the issues more, not less, deserving of attention.

Should there be a house rule that all products available for hard dollars must be paid in cash by the manager even though client soft dollars would be acceptable to the vendor? If not all products, what should the percentage be? Should senior approval be required in advance on a case-by-case basis? Should a review be conducted after the fact so policy can be corrected for application to future situations? Those who make the allocation decisions must have a high degree of personal integrity, know the brokerage business, evaluate the research, and be sensitive to differing customer objectives and needs. Reviewing what the law says at any given time may be useful, but the law does not purport to answer an ethical question—only to draw a practical line and define gross overreaching. Ethics, too, can dictate a choice of a decision because it is practical. Rough justice is workable and often desirable, as in the case of Mrs. Palsgraf's injury from the exploded fireworks. There may be practical reasons for saying here, "If the product costs less than $500, we will not worry about it; we'll pay our or the client's dollars depending on our sense of the substance and breadth of service without the hard dollar aspect being the swing factor." When the question involves broker selection by the pension fund, whether or not the item is commercially available seems a matter of indifference as long as the pension plan, and not the sponsoring corporation, benefits from the soft dollar purchase and the plan's self-interest has not shadowed a wiser use of the brokerage.

An investment manager is a sheepdog policing wandering lambs. What may seem to be an insignificant amount of commissions in a year can actually be a very large percentage during a year of substantially lower turnover. A commitment to meet such payments can be contrary to the interests of the group that needs the most protection and that relies on the pension committee and the investment manager to provide that protection.

As the trading turmoil develops and new imaginative devices are offered, there will be a greater need for ethical training for people making decisions in increasingly complex areas. They alone may be able to find an ethical solution. As in other sports, training improves performance.

Chapter 11

The North Will Rise Again
Bypassed Communities and Free Trade

With the transferability of technology and the internationalization of information, countries with traditionally protected industries routinely lose their national superiority in one group of products to some other country that develops a better or less expensive way of producing a specific industrial or agricultural product or service. The pressure to minimize costs has shifted major production facilities from our own country to a series of countries that were previously thought to be inadequately industrialized. With the impetus of the free trade patterns developed since World War II, occupational changes have accelerated. Even in the Soviet Union more jobs are being made available in the service industry while fewer are to be available in agriculture and production industries, due to mechanization and global decentralization. The communities that have been left behind, both in the sense of geographical communities and communities of workers with obsolete skills, have sought political solutions without a great deal of success. As competing nations respond, protectionism can have a whiplash effect: the complexity of the new relationship tends to create new partisans whose newly found financial well-being can be adversely affected by the restrictions needed to protect modern-day blacksmiths.

These pressures have presented particularly acute problems for the trade union movement, whose membership has been directly and adversely affected. Recently it has been seeking new ways to utilize the investment power of large pension and union welfare funds to help protect jobs, substituting a "do-it-yourself" technique for a lack of government aid.[XI-1]

Jointly managed (employer/employee) pension funds, often multiemployer funds, are a readily available tool for a particular industry. Union leaders serving on a pension committee can urge the plan to take into account the need to create and protect jobs when formulating policy and selecting specific investments.[XI-2]

We turn to a small institutional investment management firm located in a bypassed community and focus in on Sarah Bennett, a senior executive as she describes the dilemma.

One of the portfolios I manage is a local bricklayers union retirement and welfare plan. This is a multiemployer plan for members of the union; company and union representatives are jointly responsible for the selection of the trustees, the managers, and investment policy. The securities are kept in bank custody and my role as investment manager is to select the securities, both bonds and stocks, as well as liquid. I work with the actuaries and meet quarterly with the committee.

Our community has a lot of unemployment and we are all interested in how to create jobs. We don't get into political issues of the type you read about, like selling heavy tar cigarettes in Africa without the Surgeon General's legend, or selling drugs that may be used incorrectly in South America. Those questions simply don't come up. It is the investment question that is at the very heart of our management. Pure and simple, it's a question of jobs. There isn't any disagreement on that. It's all very well to say that the worker's retirements are protected because vested benefits under the plans are fully funded, but that doesn't do much good for someone who is fifty-five years old, has seven more years to work before retiring, and whose job is at risk. Where will they get a job to cover those seven years? As a matter of fact, without jobs for these people our firm wouldn't be able to exist.

We're not like lawyers who make money even on a bankrupt client. If our clients fail, we have to close up shop and start again somewhere else. So I'm on the lookout to build jobs for my clients, investing local funds in local shopping centers and new construction that can, of course, use brick rather than poured concrete. There isn't a lot of that, and I supplement my search for new construction with high yielding industrial revenue bonds issued by the nearby counties that are trying to bring in new business. Stocks from some of the machine tool companies that have been here for years have a good yield and do double duty. I reduce the risks, too, by buying their short-term commercial paper.

Recently, with new businesses being started by graduates of the state's universities, we've been able to build plants for companies with real potential for future growth, like genetic engineering, solar power, and personal computer software. Loans and tax exemptions have encouraged new hotshot technical companies with big ideas, and a lot of recent graduates want to stay in this area. The fund buys the county's bonds and the companies' stocks. A few of our stocks now have a national market; the others are handled locally. Some are private placements that we carry on the books at cost. Overall, the yield is quite good and the portfolio is obviously suited to the needs of the area and the members.

I don't mean that we are investing for charity or anything like that. The bricklayers are a little different in their need for construction investments, but all union and corporate retirement plans have the same need to support local industry during this dip. You can imagine how they would feel if we sent their hard-earned dollars to help build a robot-driven factory to produce machine tools in Korea. That is obviously a silly example, but nonetheless close to home. They want to know in advance about the labor relations of any company we select, as well as where the company's business is done and what it is. It isn't that we have to invest only in companies that are in the construction business and utilize brick. Obviously there are suppliers and customers of all sorts, like a company in the pizza business that is opening a store in a shopping center. They understand all about that and we do a lot of research.

You asked if we have had losses. Well, sure, everyone does. Even some stocks listed on the New York Stock Exchange go into the tank. When we buy privately placed securities in a small company, we usually buy their bonds rather than stocks to keep down the risk. Anyway, as you see, we are very much oriented towards our customers' needs and take more than numbers into account. We address the real needs of the people who are involved.

Bennett has identified several competing interests:

- The beneficiaries of the pension trust
- The community
- Employed and unemployed members of the union
- Families of the members
- Companies that employ members in the local area
- Customers of employers of union members
- New businesses in the area that may generate jobs

Since the pension beneficiaries rely on Bennett's expertise and pay her fees, they should receive her primary attention. In light of this fact, we must consider whether she is using her professional skills in a manner that befits her role. She is producing an investment program that is quite different from the program we would expect. She has tough choices to make. We can identify a number of specific risks to the retirement benefits, as she presumably can, but she is probably correct: the major risk in this situation is a mortal one. If the community fails due to lack of economic stimulation, pension security also fails. Bennett believes that the chance to increase job opportunities in the community warrants taking a major risk.

Does Bennett have the right to make such a policy judgment? The union and company officials who are her client contacts appear to support her efforts to create new jobs, but what of the sixty-year-old worker whose pension is put at risk by risky investments of the pension fund? There does not appear to be any likely benefit to the worker from a plebiscite of union members and beneficiaries. Most younger workers would select an improvement in the outlook for local bricklaying jobs over the cost of some remote retirement package. The persons most at risk—the retirees and those close to retirement—would be outvoted. Even if the workers were given an adequate explanation of the alternatives and permitted to participate in the decision, it is possible that there would be a division in the way they identify, prioritize, and reconcile conflicting considerations. In deciding whether or not to support Bennett's plan, members will be influenced by their families, the number of years they must work before reaching retirement, their marketable skills, the likelihood of finding another job with those skills, and whether they believe the job-building program will succeed. Asking for unbiased (and effective) communication of the options involved in the plan is like asking for the moon. Realistically viewed, it is unlikely that holding a plebiscite would produce reasoned and farsighted comments from the members. In light of this, Bennett's professional intervention may be the best that can be done to reconcile these varied concerns.

However, her decision to create jobs right now at the risk of a viable retirement fund must be reexamined. Before choosing to submit to the strong outside coercive forces from the community, local companies, and the self-interest of her own firm to create jobs, Bennett needs to step back and test why she is comfortable with the result of her decision. Some of the activity taking place in the portfolio helps jobs or retirement, but not both. Can she really justify the pension fund's investment in tax-exempt bonds of the local county since the pension fund pays no taxes, and the bonds almost certainly have a lower yield for their particular risk than would a taxable security of similar quality? It is improbable that private placement bonds in local companies are of sufficient quality to ensure retirement benefits in light of the community's shaky financial situation. Purchasing commercial paper from risky companies is always dangerous, despite the short term. The marketable securities of the new high-tech companies should be reviewed with particular care. Shopping center investment can be nonliquid and of low quality. Credits are not sufficiently discussed for us to have any sense that adequate professionalism is in fact being brought to bear on the issue. One also wonders if the social considerations have been properly evaluated.

What are the ethical points of reference to improve this situation? Could investments be selected that would both improve the financial or social well-being of the affected individuals in the short-term and enhance the future of the community as well? Can self-respect (the internal compass) be achieved by the decision? Can so-called "moral imagination" add a dimension to the analysis and conclusions? Would it be possible to manage the portfolio without subsidizing the county (through the purchase of county bonds) while launching a strong public relations effort to create jobs in the community? How can she diversify the assets of all pension trusts under her management among securities of higher quality without making her clients mad? The first answer is: slowly. She could extend a specific invitation to her pension committee to advise her on local criteria to be used in selecting securities *if and when* there are two or more equally attractive candidates for the portfolio. That invitation assumes a policy that is not yet here, but might not be challenged. This policy would probably result in geographical diversification of securities as opposed to the current riskier geographic concentration of securities. The diversification can damage the community, we hear, so she must do something about that promptly. A *pro bono* initiative by Bennett could call the attention of investment managers outside the area to the attraction of local companies: a fact that may otherwise be missed by a manager concentrating elsewhere. In turn she could learn more about the opportunities in their areas. The trade-off could benefit both clienteles and help solve the problem that Bennett is working out by creating greater diversification for all equivalent retirement funds, perhaps even through a pooled fund.

The beneficiaries' assets are paying the investment management fee, and the beneficiaries are bearing the risk of loss. As their rights are technically infringed upon by Bennett's current high risk, geographically concentrated portfolio, we need to ask whether the "moral imagination" alternative avoids this without ignoring the claims of those who contribute to the portfolio through their daily work.

Often, a choice that benefits one group infringes on another group's rights. We are continually challenged to make decisions that minimally infringe on the rights of all involved groups. If no such course of action can be identified, we have to assign a priority to one alternative; in this case is it to jobs or pensions? Do priorities depend on the number of people affected? On the degree to which they are affected by the policy? On their ability or lack of ability to fend for themselves?

Are all of the involved groups being treated fairly and equally? Are the interests of the competing claimants as homogeneous as Bennett indicated, or can more subtle lines be drawn to help various groups more appropriately and better benefit all? In terms of issues, we need to resolve the conflicting goals of jobs and retirement benefits. The power count is clearly on the side of jobs (union and management trustees, younger workers and their families, and the community all favor jobs). Yet the fiduciary must respond to those who rely on the manager's representation of their interests: older workers whose dependence on the pension is critical. Paternalism, the complement of reliance, cannot be delegated back via beneficiary participation: the beneficiaries have limited understanding of the issues and must not be subjected to manipulation and peer coercion.

Bennett could refuse to adhere to the local job-creating script as written by her client. To continue as is can be a violation of her responsibilities. Since her self-respect and integrity are at issue in the present situation, she must find a way out. Yet to undo current security holdings without inviting termination by the union/management trustees requires Bennett to know her fiduciary goals. At least privately, she must be able to acknowledge personal responsibility for any harm caused by her future actions while reinforcing her self-esteem through the knowledge that she is doing her best for those affected by the situation. She does not need to blatantly tell the industry and union trustees that their job priority decision is wrong; by doing so she would risk being fired, unnecessarily frighten people, gain publicity that could alert litigious sixty-year-old beneficiaries and take business away from her, probably passing it to a less sensitive manager. The best course of action seems to be to chip away at the problem piece-by-piece, gradually making her goals of quality and diversification for the stock portfolio public, and establishing the underpinning for safer retirement benefits at the same time she seeks outside investment and more jobs in the county.

By following this two-layer course of action Bennett and her clients are well on their way to a solution that will most greatly benefit all of the involved parties. Stating the question of jobs versus pensions we provide a partial answer.

Chapter 12

The Boesky Syndrome
What is Wrong with Using Hot Information?

Despite all the recent indictments, arrests, handcuffs, headlines, fines, and prison terms there is still little public understanding of why the use of insider information is ethically wrong. It takes the image of hundreds of thousands of dollars being passed to the source of insider information in an alley off Wall Street to dramatize the aspects of bribery, embezzlement, and corporate espionage.

Most cases involving the use of insider information are less sensational than those of Ivan Boesky, Dennis Levine, and the like; they may never reach the courts and thus seem harder to categorize.

Consider the process in which a board of directors decides to substantially raise the dividend for the company based on a surprisingly good report of sales and profits. One director, Betty Duke, excuses herself during a coffee break and instructs a broker to buy stock in the company. Using knowledge that she "owns" only because her duties include representing the shareholders, she is personally profiting in a transaction with one of her constituents, a selling shareholder who lacks similar knowledge. She did not, however, induce that shareholder to sell, and the shareholder would have sold anyway as it was an unsolicited transaction, receiving the same dollars as from another buyer. No one can complain. No one was hurt. Or is that so? Theft, with or without "damage," is wrong under most ethical tests. Was this theft?

As a matter of public policy, the interests of the shareholders as a class come before the self-interest of this director, whose job is to represent the shareholders' interest. Proof of harm to the specific shareholder who sold the shares that this director bought cannot be the ethical test: the director might win! Looking at it another way, one might say that a policy against directors personally profiting from nonpublic corporate information reflects a general ethical need to address events involving the self-interest of directors. Otherwise, directors would have an undesirable incentive to keep important news from their shareholders rather than disclose such news. So viewed, the public interest is harmed by the director's preemption of the investment opportunity.

Would the conclusion differ if that company's president, Marcus Flyte, bought a good deal of the company's stock before presenting to the directors a proposal to raise the dividend? Theoretically, at the time of the stock purchase there would have been uncertainty, which was not the case after the vote when Duke acted. It is not very convincing for the president to argue that the purchase was not tied to the board's dividend decision, especially if the board did raise the dividend. The utilitarian rule, "the greatest good for the greatest number," excludes the self-interest of the decision maker as a justifiable motive, leading us to the benchmarks that shareholders as a whole are better off if there is disclosure; insiders should not act on undisclosed information since that would be a deterrent to disclosure. This view is reinforced from a "rights" perspective; the shareholders' rights to material information would be infringed upon if agents put their own personal interests ahead of the shareholders' interest. The ethical linchpin here is the duty of the management to work for the shareholders.

Is it different if Duke sells her mother's stock in the company when she learns at a board meeting of an unexpected drop in earnings of such significance that the regular dividend will have to be omitted? Does her professional duty only apply to her own transactions? Does it apply only to transactions with existing stockholders? Or does it extend to the purchaser of her mother's shares? Such distinctions sound legalistic, not ethical. The director's duty cannot be subordinated to her self-interest in either case. Giving her mother the benefit of her knowledge does not change the irresponsibility.[XII-1]

Let's carry the scenario a step further. If Flyte makes no personal security transactions but tells a security analyst as a step in disseminating the information, is the analyst limited in the actions he or she can take? Is it fair to restrict the actions of people who are paid to sift information, dig deeply, and give advice? Aren't financial analysts (who talk to company officials and their customers) part of the important process of locating and disseminating material information?

The following interview is with a security analyst for a large investment manager, Mary Barnard.

We have established a number of very careful rules about the use of inside information. The first issue is to establish whether the information is really inside information, and this is sometimes a little hard to know. There are always so many rumors floating around, though information and rumors are not the same thing. We analysts have a role analogous to a lawyer's role as "officer of the court;" we are, so to speak, officers of the securities markets. Assuming that it is hard information and I have heard it in confidence, I need to decide if it will really have an impact on the price of the stock or if it is just another detail whose importance is tied to knowing the whole picture. If it is not itself a headline item my using it will not distort the market. If it were a headline item, a "smoking gun", and I heard it in confidence from the director, I would keep the confidence and not use the information any more than the director should. That is how our internal rules work, as you see from this policy we have developed on insider information.

Policy on Insider Information
1. Our firm doesn't use material inside information concerning the value or price of stocks for making decisions in accounts.
2. If you receive such information don't use it and don't spread the news. Don't tell your client. Don't even tell your boss. Keep them free and able to use public information while you discuss a constructive course of action with our lawyers.
3. With the door closed, talk it out with somebody in the legal department to see if there is really a problem. Did the information come from the company on a private basis so you are bound by the same restrictions and loyalties that bind your source? Is it still private? Is it really important information or is it just a minor detail? Would it in itself swing your judgment of the stock one way or the other?
4. If there is a problem, work out a way to let our client come out as well as if we hadn't received the prohibited information.
5. Remember, brokers can provide tips, true or untrue, in order to block our actions while they buy or sell under their own plan. It's better for our clients if you stop the person from telling you the tip before you hear it.

One time we had some important insider information about a plant closing by a company we bought for one of our big clients. We got a specific reporter to investigate the area. It wasn't a big news story, but she did investigate it and when the details appeared in the paper we got rid of the stock. We didn't tell the client that

101

we had gone through all of this mickey mouse business, and it would seem there ought to be better ways of doing that. We could have spread the rumor ourselves, but then everyone except our client could benefit. We could have tried to get the company to release it. I suppose we could have called a press conference, but we wouldn't be warmly received the next time we visited the company.

It is very rare that a single piece of news, whether public or private, could swing our decision; we are long-term investors and something that may change the stock price for a few days doesn't interest us in the same way it would an arbitrageur. A good detail pushes me in one direction or the other or supports my current conclusion. We sometimes call that "mosaic information" because it's just another little piece to fit in and you have to have a lot of pieces to create the picture.

When you see news stories about insider information, you get the sense that government policy dictates that everybody is supposed to have the same amount of information. I don't see how that is ever possible. Bribing someone at the company to pass on confidential information to you is one thing, but what if somebody at the company calls you and says, "we just filed a report and on page ninety-three you'll find something that might be of interest to you." What do you do about that if it's big? It isn't fair to your customers to be so much of a prude that you ignore your responsibilities to them.

I worked in a bank once, before all of these lawsuits on insider information, and we used to argue about our duty to our trust beneficiaries coming first. Let's say you came across some piece of important new information about the British oil reserves off Scotland while visiting a foreign supplier to a drilling company. Does that mean you couldn't add to your stock in the drilling company? Do you have the obligation to go beyond the law? Or let's say you saw a tanker in a shipyard and the tanker was badly damaged and you knew it had never been reported. Should you let the trust beneficiaries who are depending on you suffer because the company's P.R. department, for one reason or another, hadn't put the news out? Or what about the small company that puts out a press release that never gets printed at all, but you were at the company the day it was released? We are hired to use our skills. If we get too tied to creating some absolutely level playing field for all investors we wouldn't be doing our job.

Actually, if everybody had the same information they would still make different judgments. Insider trades by management are required to be reported, and you see some managers buying and some of them selling. They have different considerations, and even if their sole consideration was making a buck some would buy and some would sell. I have to admit that isn't always true— say if there were a real life discovery like Crest toothpaste by Procter and Gamble, a real breakthrough in dental care beyond anything in the past. Or finding that the earnings reports were phonied-up by management at Equity Funding. We may have efficient markets but they don't take into account the surprises outside of the mainstream information. And of course they cannot.

I still have a lot of trouble figuring out how to tackle information of this kind, except to do what our legal eagles tell me is permissible.

Let's say I come across information on a company that says the whole crowd is crooked and, as Ray Dirks did with Equity Funding, I go to the S.E.C. and tell them what I've learned and they don't do anything about it. Am I supposed to let my client stay in the stock or sell them out? That's crazy. I can't call a press conference: I could get sued for slander and so could the firm. I can't just do nothing, let my customers swing in the wind. My customers look to me to take care of them and use my best investment judgment.

Even if my information isn't 100 percent accurate I can't blank out my awareness of this kind of situation. So what I would do is sell, unless the legal department said this was against the law. I have a responsibility to the firm not to violate the law, and our customers certainly can't expect us to go to jail to make a few dollars profit for them. But isn't the correct line of reasoning to do what's in the interest of the people paying us unless this is somehow impossible? On the other hand, the S.E.C. actually went after Ray Dirks for selling out his customers' shares in Equity Funding!

That still doesn't answer the question of what ethical reasons would lead me to identify an insider information problem in the first place. As an analyst, my job is to turn up information that nobody else has, to see something that nobody else sees that can affect the future. I don't mean industrial espionage. I mean legitimate and hard analytical work like asking the right questions and being smart enough (or lucky enough) to see how it all fits with everything else I know.

Just to make it clear how silly all this is, if I can't tell anybody about, say, the Equity Funding fraud, and I can't do anything to get my clients out of it, that means I have to watch other clients buying the stock when I know the earnings are phony, that Equity Funding is a two-dimensional illusion, like the Potemkin Village. I don't understand that at all.

There is a real social problem when legal sanctions do not have the underpinning of ethical perspectives. Uninformed people with the best of intentions can push in contrary directions; informed people may look for exceptions and excuses that undercut public policy. This is especially true of those who are not well-intentioned, feel no social pressure, and run yellow lights—weighing only the cost of any sanctions against their own economic benefit.

The ethical basis of insider information prohibitions can be compared with the transcendent perception that the physical environment may be a "party" to management decisions. Consider the situation in which a mining company has exploitation rights[XII-2] with the consent of a foreign government, operates in a place in which the population is minimal, and leaves behind a great scar on the earth. No one complains. Without question, many of us would prefer that the scar be repaired without regard to the question of costs or benefits. The company's controller has the mission of guarding shareholders' money from unnecessary expenditures. The phrase "physical environment" helps. It introduces the concept of humanity's stewardship, our need to respect the interests of future generations. Narrowly, the earth's resources and other living things, both vegetable and animal, need protection and consideration in order to provide the resources that may be required to meet unknown future needs.[XII-3] Carrying this line of reasoning to the financial markets, a transcendent ethic is that the participants in the markets should help justify public confidence in those markets—manipulation is bad—advance information should be widely available for early evaluation. This helps the solvency of the specialist on the floor of the exchange and it helps the market remain orderly and warrant the confidence of investors.

This concept condemns more than bribery, embezzlement of ideas, and corporate espionage. It reorders the actions of directors who would sell their own stock before releasing negative, undisclosed information. It helps us see the individuals on the other side of the transactions that take place on exchange, not as faceless but as representative of all who should have been told. It imposes an obligation on the directors to uphold the integrity of the market in which their companies' stock trades: the corporation has chosen to be listed on the Exchange and thereby the directors assumed an obligation to be fair to brokers, dealers, issuers, and customers of the Exchange. In turn, as an analyst Barnard, acting as a representative for the shareholders, has a similar obligation. This is reinforced in a self-interest rationale that her customers cannot trade on insider information without others trading on it against them.

The legal system's conclusion of where the line between proper and prohibited conduct is to be drawn is not the same question. The law may or may not go as far as ethics. As we have seen in the case of the explosion of the firecrackers on the Long Island Railroad, courts draw lines of liability for damages based on practical foreseeability of harmful consequences. That does not mean that it is ethical to take the chance of hurting somebody if the one who is hurt is not "foreseeable." You may falsely shout "fire" in a crowded theatre. Everyone exits in an orderly fashion. The fire truck comes and finds no fire. Returning to the station house the truck hits a pedestrian. You may not be liable for that accident in a court of law, but from an ethical point of view you have set in motion an irresponsible and powerful wave that brings unknown harm to unidentified individuals. And someone was hurt. It may seem too much to carry that point over to insider information, unless we remind ourselves that the integrity of the marketplace has an irreplaceable value.

Consider the following two cases:

1) A brokerage house learns that its investment banking client has suffered an unannounced grave loss that may or may not be covered by insurance. At the time the security is on its retail "buy list" and the account representatives, not knowing of the losses, recommend its purchase. To sell out the retail customers' stock means trading on information that the company has withheld from the public. Inaction prejudices its retail customers. The trap set by the dual relationship must be deactivated. Will the brokerage house's ethical obligation to both the retail customer and the integrity of the marketplace be dealt with if it removes the security from the "buy list" without explaining why, so that no new purchases will occur and no harm will be created by silence? It is of some help, but it is incomplete: the retail customers will still be holding a stock they will wish they had sold. Are both objectives achieved through an instruction that no purchases or sales are to be made until further notice? That may improperly block the innocent sale. Are there other steps that can be taken? What if a new analyst were assigned to the company on a temporary basis in order to do a special review? If the new analyst recommends a sale, that would solve the problem, but it may look like a cover-up for a decision to use the inside information. Whether imposing a Chinese wall of insulation between the broker's inside information and the new decision maker's

analysis is an adequate response to this situation depends on the credibility of the policy. In fact, the brokerage firm as an entity knows the harm from doing nothing, and at the same time has an obligation not to use the information for private gain. The only way out would seem to be to decline in advance to try to serve two masters: investment banking customers and investors. That was how investment counsel became organized. A less radical solution would be to never make a recommendation on the stocks of investment banking customers—and to tell the investors.

2) At a cocktail party on Tuesday night a reporter with a large following tells a portfolio manager he is completing a story that is going to attack the self-dealing of top management in a specific large corporation and expects to get the story out that week. The portfolio manager knows it will be a serious story, and that the price of the stock will be adversely affected for a long time. Where does the manager go from here? Assume that the manager has investment discretion over accounts and there has been no rumor of any management self-dealing. The source is not the company. The information did not come by theft. The story may not be true. The story may never appear. Is the manager's duty to retain the reporter's information and not use the information in a way that damages public confidence in reporters? Was the information disclosed in confidence by a reporter the manager had helped in the past? Is the reporter's sobriety relevant? It would be manipulative for the reporter to sell short the company's stock before the story appears: is the manager bound by the same standard? Is there a way of reconciling these different interests without material disadvantage to any of the parties? If there is a current program in place for buying the stock, that should be stopped. As physicians say, *primum non nocere:* the first step is to avoid positive action that creates harm. Prior clearance of all trades in that stock by a senior officer could be required, so that on a case-by-case basis all purchases can be blocked and planned sales that had nothing to do with the inside information can go through.

*　　*　　*　　*　　*

It was one thing for Barnard to say that the customer could not expect the loyalty required by the fiduciary relationship to extend to violating the security laws. Beyond that, does an analyst have a right to exceed the security laws to protect the integrity of the marketplace despite losing legitimate opportunities for the investment management client? What if the judgment is wrong: inaction when action would not have violated the security laws, or the information turns out subsequently not to be significant or to have been disclosed?

The goal is to be on the same wavelength as the clients so that they expect a good faith judgment. Then policy can be broader than the current laws. Client communication can get at the root of the public policy and explain its substance and the benefit of aboveboard markets. In turn, such involvement by the clients can support and reinforce the growth of an ethical bias not just on the part of a manager like Barnard but across the board. It might even be good business.

Chapter 13

The Consent of the Governed
Leading and Misleading

Governance of corporations can become Byzantine, convoluted, and coercive, sometimes inadvertently and unwittingly. Time pressures, poorly thought-out procedures, mechanical applications of logic, and rules can be the culprits. A good manager prevents this from happening.

In this chapter we return to Massachusetts Conglomerates and examine its recent merger with New Hampshire Systems, Inc. (NHSI), a company with which it had a control relationship for several years. At the heart of the transaction, the president of MassCon, Martin Holyoke, discusses the transaction and the part played by two colleagues, Stan Smith and Mel Dean.

We originally bought into NHSI with the thought that we needed a good solid supply relationship for that end of our business. It was a friendly arrangement with the people over there and we limited purchases of their stock to bring us up to 51 percent. That was five years ago. We reorganized the NHSI board, which had thirteen directors, put five MassCon people on, plus Mel Dean, one of the investment banking guys who had worked with us in the original negotiation and tender offer. We left the management team intact. It all worked very well and NHSI was making a good deal of money. Two years ago, Sam Cruz, their C.E.O., retired and we sent over Stan Smith, one of our senior management people, to run the company and he became a director.

As you know, our plan to acquire Deer Field Tool didn't work out. So, we thought about other uses for our cash and decided to consolidate our holding, merging NHSI into MassCon. I had two of our people who are on the NHSI board do a feasibility study and they said it would be financially attractive for us at any price up to $24 a share. The stock was then trading at $14 a share and I okayed a range of $20-21 at our executive committee meeting. That afternoon I called Stan Smith, told him about the merger idea, and gave him the $20-21 figure for the NHSI board meeting that was coming up. We also sent out a press release saying that the two companies were in negotiation, so our people would not jump the gun on personal stock trades, what with the spread between $14 and $20. Inside information was one of the concerns of our legal department. Actually, that's how I got the $21 figure: 50 percent appreciation seemed like a damn good deal for those shareholders without getting into a lot of statistics.

A special meeting of their board was set for a Monday morning, ten days later. We had Stan reach all of the outside directors and explain the deal right away. I also told him to get Mel Dean, our banker, to have his firm write up the appraisal and pay him the standard fee for that kind of thing. He had all the back-up documentation from five years ago (when we got control) and through his period as a director, so it was no sweat except for the timing.

That was the script. Mel assigned the job to two people at his firm. They did the review, went over fluctuations of the price of NHSI, sent someone out to look at the plants, and wrote it up. They finished it on the weekend and Mel met with the senior guy before the meeting Monday morning. The fee came to $150,000 which was pretty heavy, but it was a tight schedule.

The NHSI board circulated Mel's opinion and agreed that everything they needed was included. Mel called me to check the price and I told him $21, so he wrote that in, signed the report, and it was made a formal part of the minutes. We were holding our MassCon board meeting at the same time, and when Stan said they were ready, we were in touch with a telephone conference call to confirm everything. When the NHSI shareholders met, about ten weeks later, there was a whopping majority for the merger.

Later, of course, there was that publicity about our internal study and the $24 price and why hadn't that been told to the NHSI people. In retrospect it is too bad, because Stan could have handled that with his own directors.

Even if we had had to put that into the NHSI proxy it could have been innocuously stated.

Well, so much for that. The merger has been a terrific success and a lot of us feel it turned out better for us than a merger with Deer Field Tool would have.

Mr. Holyoke seems to have left out a few pertinent points. For instance, what are the competing claims?

- The NHSI management want to protect and continue the status quo, including their employment.
- The NHSI shareholders want the highest price for their shares if there is to be a cash transaction; they want a good exchange if they are to become shareholders of MassCon.
- MassCon's management and shareholders want to pay the lowest feasible price for NHSI shares; MassCon is apparently only interested in a cash transaction rather than an exchange.

Continued employment of the NHSI management. In light of the past relationship between NHSI and MassCon, the NHSI management would not seem to have any serious worries about staying on. As MassCon has had 51 percent of the stock and a majority of the board, it has already had the practical power of making any management changes it wants to. However, NHSI's management is being showcased in this transaction and their skill or lack of it in achieving what MassCon wants will be obvious. They will wish to handle themselves so as to gain MassCon approval or at least avoid disapproval.

Value to the NHSI shareholders. The 49 percent minority has little power. MassCon holds most of the power with the simple 51 percent majority. But some public shareholders must agree to the merger if it is to be effective; a minority has the power to institute litigation if there is a waste of corporate assets by the management. Realistically, however, the minority has few options aside from accepting what MassCon offers, since there will be no unanimous bloc. Since the original tender, NHSI has apparently done well, with the fundamental value of the NHSI stock rising to at least $24 according to the MassCon committee of NHSI experts.

This combination of circumstances puts a burden on the managements of both companies to deal fairly with the minority shareholders. Holyoke's reference to bad publicity triggered further investigation: the original request for tenders five years before was also at a price of $21; and the original tender offer was presented in combination with a purchase of treasury shares directly from NHSI, so only 25 percent of the publicly tendered shares were acquired. MassCon limited the number of shares it would accept. The tender was substantially oversubscribed. The market price of $14 at the time of this second transaction reflects the lack of control

NHSI shareholders had over their destiny. The current offer of $21 may be based less on a 50 percent appreciation for the shareholders, as Holyoke remembered, than it was on dusting off the old offer, despite higher current value and excellent prospects.

How much effort must a well-informed majority make to deal fairly with an ill-informed minority? Was the procedure used by MassCon fair? Was the price fair? That the legal counsel of MassCon cleared the process and the price is not the end but a possible beginning of the ethical inquiry. There is an obligation to go beyond the minimal rights of those who are underrepresented and inadequately informed. If the notion of fair allocation interferes with MassCon's philosophy of entrepreneurship, risk taking, innovation, and productivity, which deserves priority? Can the rights of the NHSI shareholders be protected without infringing upon the rights of MassCon shareholders who have to bear the extra cost of a price over $21?

Without resolving these general issues we can conclude that in his communication with Stan Smith, Holyoke deliberately created the false impression that the feasibility study had come up with a price of $21 a share as the basis of a fair offer, supported by the former price for tenders, the oversubscription at the time, and the current market price of $14. Perhaps an ethical case can be made for the $21 price. If we look only at the consequences of our acts, the merger might be justified as beneficial on many sides, including elimination of the difficulties for NHSI shareholders ever to realize a proper price in the market, and the need of a management to identify and act in the self-interest of its company. If only the facts had been put on the table. What actually occurred suggests a potential loss of confidence between executives of this new NHSI division and top MassCon management: in misleading Smith to believe the price reached in the feasibility study was $21 Holyoke was lying. Lying to your subordinates is hardly acceptable behavior under any Code of Managers' Conduct. In addition, the public was lied to when the press release stated that "negotiations" were occurring. This was untrue because the NHSI management was not negotiating, not identifying and acting in the self-interest of all of its shareholders, but was simply going through a ratification procedure. Even the appraisal had the value left blank for Holyoke and Dean to fill in.

Management by objective is a very important tool for executives. It provides a degree of certainty and a method of evaluation and accountability to all concerned. But early in life most of us learned that the propriety of means must be judged on their own. Whether we call that conclusion "ethics," "good management," or something else, good ends and bad means make a poor combination. Here, to be a good manager and justify his actions as ethical, Holyoke would have to identify overwhelming factors to suspend truth-telling as a prerequisite to the communication and the negotiation. Was Holyoke acting to produce the greatest good for the greatest number? He saw himself as Solomon, entitled to decide for the minority shareholders, and he then carried out his conclusion in the most expedient way.

Even if we were to be convinced that $21 is a fair price, can such multilayered misdirection by management be tolerated as a precedent?[XIII-1]

Chapter 14

Winning With Someone Else's Money
Being Parochial; Being Professional

The success of the American system of privately blended pension plans reflects carrots (tax deductions for contributions) and sticks (a requirement to phase in the full funding of plans with defined benefits). The Employee Retirement Income Security Act (E.R.I.S.A.), despite administrative problems, has proved an extremely constructive force in accelerating the expansion of secured benefits since its enactment in 1974. It is founded on an ethical principle that retirement income has a social priority. The Act and Rules issued by the U.S. Department of Labor detail ways to achieve that objective. Those details are not necessarily the limits for the ethical manager, but the manager must understand the details of administration to know whether an "ethical decision" works as planned.

Under E.R.I.S.A., sponsors chose between two types of plans—plans to provide a defined employee benefit and plans that define the sponsor's contribution. A defined benefit plan requires an actuary to determine the sponsor contribution required for each particular year to meet the benefit, which is often tied by formula to the high end of an employee's salary history. The actuary looks at the profile of current asset values, prospective beneficiaries at different times, and future interest rate probabilities. A manager could then meet the funding target provided by the actuary by investing in fixed-income securities, guaranteed insurance contracts, and other "immunizing" investment techniques designed to match the liabilities and the assets. In general, however, managers do not seek simply to match performance to the actuarial projection. Rather, they seek superior performance as a cushion, with the expectation that such success could benefit the corporation and its employees by anticipating expanded benefits and permitting reduced future contributions. As payment on retirement of the defined benefit, which is generally tied to a salary-based formula, is part of the employment contract between the employee and the sponsoring corporation, any underfunding of vested payments has to be met by the corporation: the plan sponsor has a continued residual obligation to pay the vested benefits. To that extent the fund is an "asset" of the sponsor; however, it is pledged as collateral under the plan.

As inflation rates expanded in the 1970s, interest rates also leaped into double digits. The pressure on costs from accelerating inflation and the high interest rates paid by corporations to borrow funds in turn made its cash tight and many corporate sponsors had difficulty meeting required pension contribution schedules. They pressed their actuaries to assume for their funding contributions future interest rates that were higher than the 5 or 6 percent historically used. The current funding contribution required on an 8 percent return on investment would be lower than if only 5 percent were to be earned in the fund, and the pressure on the corporation's current cash would be less significant.

Some corporations that found these changes to be an inadequate solution to their cash flow pressures terminated their defined benefit plans entirely, often replacing them with plans based on a *defined contribution* by the corporation. A typical defined contribution plan, such as a percent of base compensation, relieves the corporation of the need to guarantee retirement amounts. Upon making this payment, the corporation is more or less off the hook if it acts in good faith. The plan may even permit employees to choose how their accounts are to be invested.

Whether or not a defined contribution plan is substituted, a sponsor's decision to terminate a defined benefit plan is implemented by transferring a fixed dollar amount equal to the present value of the vested benefits due the participants. Accurate interest rate expectations in the future are important to correctly determine present value. If the plan is underfunded the sponsor may have to dig into its pockets; on the other hand if the value of assets of the plan exceeds the requirements of the defined benefit, the corporation has been legally entitled to recapture them.[XIV-1]

The termination of a defined benefit plan by Consolidated Media Enterprises (CME) is discussed below by Clarence Monte, the company's president.

In the media business, there have been a lot of mergers and consolidations over the years. We have, nevertheless, been able to stay independent and our independence has attracted a lot of good people to work here.

We were recently approached with a merger proposal by a foreign raider, REGA. It was our inventory of copyrighted materials that REGA was after, not a big cash pool. We are still sweeping up the broken glass, but we won. Our ace in the hole was the Snyder family, which founded CME and held one-third of the shares. They were willing to sell out to anyone if they could get a big enough offer, and that would be the end of the company. But we had the inside track.

We worked out a deal with the Snyders and then figured out how to handle the payment. It was really quite simple. Short-term interest rates were at 18 percent when we changed the interest rate assumed on the pension plan from 6 percent to 15 percent, which the actuaries went along with. This showed that the plan was in an overfunded position and we terminated the plan. We issued lump sum settlements to the pension beneficiaries, equal to the present value of the accrued benefits, using the same 15 percent interest rate assumption. That set of computations gave the plan a $9 million surplus that we repatriated to CME. Looking back, 15 percent seems high, but at the time the country had almost gone to 20 percent in terms of interest rates.

For the future, we expanded the existing profit-sharing plan, amending it to permit investment in CME securities—up to half of its assets. We have had the profit-sharing plan as a supplement to the pension plan for a long time, but it was not very significant. Last, but not least, we established an employee bonus plan to take over the balance of the block of the stock we had acquired from the Snyders. As far as the risks are concerned, we will all be sharing them. One for all and all for one!

More than that, we will be out from under the U.S. Pension Benefit Guaranty Agency (P.B.G.C.), which issues pension benefits for bankrupt plans by taxing the solvent companies like us. We had talked for a long time about getting rid of the defined benefits plan as the P.B.G.C. insurance premiums have been going up and seemed to be going higher in order to cover the underfunded retirement plans of other companies. If it had been just insurance for our own funding that would be one thing, but it went against the grain to assist dropouts who had not done the necessary funding over the years. So those insurance costs will no longer be part of our overhead. That will put money into the hands of the employees, too.

Starting from the point of pragmatism, management won; starting from practical ethics, let's sort out the separate interests: first, who won and who lost and then get at the questions of rights and fairness.

Obviously, in order to determine the rights that are involved in the case and could potentially be infringed upon, it is necessary to identify the persons who are affected by CME's actions and decisions. (Remember not to disregard any hunch you may have about what is fair, but also test its validity!)

There is the Snyder family. Long-term shareholders have a right to change their commitment to a company. It is logical that family members' interests would differ over time. The family is no longer active in management. Its shares are undoubtedly dispersed among many different trusts with different advisers who are pressing for portfolio diversification. But what consequences flow from the Snyders' years of standing fast with CME? Were there consequent expectations on the part of other shareholders and reliance by them that the stability and family support would continue? If public shareholders had been led to believe the Snyder family was still a key to CME, should the Snyders have alerted the public about prospective withdrawal plans so the shareholders could act in their own best interest? We know Monte was aware of the Snyder family's interest in selling, so there was some information that could have been communicated to public shareholders. Was it? Whether and how to release this information would have to be weighed against the possibility of jeopardizing CME's independence by increasing the number of competitors for the block.

Second, we must consider the shareholders who underwrite the premium payment by CME to the Snyders. We usually think of "greenmail" when the outsider holds up the company. The company here seems to have taken the initiative. Assuming that "greenmail" premiums paid to minorities who threaten management are questionable, does this situation differ in substance? Would the premium have been "greenmail" if paid to the Snyders' successors? Is it a premium reasonably appropriate to the market value of such a substantial block?

Next, there are the beneficiaries of the pension trust. They are entitled to their legal rights to receive vested benefits. A 15 percent interest rate projection for purposes of lump sum payments was a bad deal for the vested beneficiaries. At that time, the 15 percent projection should have been seen as excessive when viewed in a fifty-year perspective. Was there an alternative, such as an annuity? Even if there was a proper annuity reflecting past contributions, what of expectancies of employees as to future contributions? While they could have been adequately addressed by the management's expansion of the profit-sharing fund, management instead coerced the trustees of the profit-sharing trust to purchase CME stock for cash in order to place control in the hands of the management, risking the viability of the profit-sharing trust. The management procedure suggests a lack of collegiality that is, at the least, troubling. Since it is a profit-sharing trust, with only a defined contribution obligation on the part of the corporation, there is no added sponsor guaranty, no underpinning. Moreover, tieing the employee's future retirement funds so much to the success of the corporation (through employment, a thrift plan, and a profit-sharing plan dominated by CME stock) contradicts any concept of a safety net. When viewed collectively, the actions make us wonder about Monte's good faith.

Finally, we must consider the employees. Before the transaction, they expected that in addition to receiving their regular salaries and wages they would receive a series of benefits, including specified retirement benefits. Those expectations were unilaterally altered. The trust agreement and plan undoubtedly gave CME the legal right to do so, but were the employees' undeniably reasonable expectations taken into account? Did the employees have a voice in management's decision to save CME's independence with the employees' assets? Were the employees given objective information to realize the risks involved in receiving a lump sum payment where adequacy was based on a future 15 percent return? Could that have been achieved? Only if an annuity could have been purchased that had the 15 percent interest figure locked in.

The motive for CME's decision to terminate the plan and transfer CME shares to the thrift plan and the profit-sharing trust is based on the need to preserve *the company's* independence. However, Monte does not make clear why the employees as a class will be better off if CME's defense is successful. Indeed, their employment might be more secure and their pension benefits more solid under REGA. On the other hand if, as we are told, REGA was just looking for the copyrighted inventory and CME would have been dissolved after REGA's takeover, vigorous defense may have been the only desirable course. But it should be examined.

We tend to take as true whatever we are told. Only if we force ourselves do most of us consider the alternative. There is a story that three worms went separately into a sand mound on the beach. When the smallest came out of the hole, it looked back at the holes and said, "there are two holes." Left to explain, the listener focuses on why it only saw two holes: shifts in sand, a perspective that blocks the view of the third hole.

The lecturer's answer is that what the worm saw, it called two holes, but it saw three holes. It lied or couldn't count. Our assumptions are often unexpressed and sometimes wrong. To get at reality we have to plan for that possibility, to avoid kidding ourselves about the facts we know and about the accuracy of others.

What of the shareholders? The sweetheart deal carried out by CME, where the Snyder block was acquired in order to thwart REGA, deprived public shareholders of the chance to sell their CME stock to REGA at a premium. We don't have enough information to know whether paying the Snyder family a premium is in the shareholders' interest or is a breach of the responsibilities entrusted to the corporate management.

A simple summary of the consequences permits an overview of the transaction.

The Snyders
● Benefitted by the transaction: a good deal.
Executives
● Benefitted by the transaction. They preserve their jobs.
Salaried employees
● Pensions threatened. The benefit may be job preservation.
Hourly employees
● Retirement system threatened. The benefit may be job preservation.
Public shareholders
● Loss of an opportunity to sell shares at a premium.
Customers
● If REGA is interested in the copyrights, presumably the product will continue to be sold, whether manufactured by CME or REGA. However, the attitude might be different and the nature of future production could be circumscribed or expanded.
Suppliers/authors
● Risks of change for them if CME were liquidated and REGA took over the publication of their works.
The Board of Directors
● The transaction benefits them to the extent they would presumably cease to be the directors of the merged corporation.
The society
● Benefits from independent printers; suffers if it tolerates manipulation.

The group most clearly benefitted on CME's side is the very group that decided to terminate the defined benefit plan and use the employees' money to acquire the key shares of CME stock in order to block REGA. The shareholders and employees are most adversely affected. Even if the result of independence is proper, it cannot be accepted as ethical when the means were coercive and selfish.

Nothing in Monte's statement supports a conclusion that his personal values played a large part in the decisions: we have to act with some consistency in light of our personal value system to build an identity. It need not be "conscience at all costs," crankiness, insistence in the vein of "do-it-our-way-and-the-public-be-damned." That is caricature. Silence and nonconfrontation are often associated with persons of integrity who recognize their limits. Integrity and professionalism seek nonconfrontation during the period in which the facts are being identified and analyzed and the team is framing the questions. A professional contends first with the concrete and the present rather than jumping in with an answer before the question is asked. Analysis of concrete facts, anticipation, communication, virtue, clarity, truthfulness, and practicality go hand in hand, reinforcing a professional's identity. Corporate policy should encourage such integrity on the part of employees.

Deliberate misrepresentation to the employees may have occurred in the CME case, but it is much more likely that confusion was caused by moving too quickly with a limited perspective urged forward by lawyer advocates and investment banking advocates—experts! *Tant pis*. This type of situation results in half-truths being communicated in jargon. The outside experts can bring in a poor sense of history of the company and, because of the speed of the transaction, there may be poor post event recall. All too often, if it's "legal" and in the interest of management a course of action is treated as desirable. In this case the board of CME even congratulates itself for its skill.

Each of us has been in a situation where we act out a role, play a part. We state an advocate's position, oversimplifying the "we" and the "they," limiting the discussion to persuasive arguments in support of our role's position. To do so is to be sophomoric, not in charge. To be professional a manager must have principles to apply when processing elusive facts and probabilities that fall short of certainty, must test the edges of things in order to know them. A professional is someone whose knowledge of principles and goals includes knowing which tools to apply to different situations. The CME board seems to have accepted Monte's statement without testing it. As a result the board members deceived themselves and may have cheated the employees. The board needed to look past the "given objective," which was to defend CME at all costs. Costs, impacts, relationships, and interests needed to be treated individually so the REGA threat could be seen from a variety of angles and a variety of responses could be identified.

A good board of directors protects management from itself.

To do so no board member should get caught up by the team spirit of the board to acquiesce with the majority rather than speak up, to say "yes" rather than make the kind of analysis that can add the unique value his or her training offers. What value does a person provide by saying "yes" to the boss? When the boss is moving to take a course of action it is the new perception that adds value: the honesty, however courteously stated, of seeing through the "emperor's clothes." The more important the context the harder it may be to stand one's ground; yet when the director's corporation is under assault it is unlikely that even one member would comfort the people threatening the corporation. Such unanimity can be a flaw. Perhaps the answer is that the very best director is the one who is a team player only as long as the team is working to meet objectives that are fair to the whole team.

Sir Thomas More[XIV-2] was most helpful to King Henry because of the clarity of his vision in concrete matters, his personal integrity, and consistent action. Ultimately, when More was offered the largest bribe of all, a place of honor in the history of his country in return for a ruling he could give only by abandoning his own vision of truth, a tragedy and simultaneous victory occurred: he was beheaded but he acted as the person the king had chosen.

We, like More, undermine or strengthen our personal integrity, flesh out our essential identity, strengthen or weaken our company by each daily decision we make on concrete matters.

Chapter 15

Play It Again, Sam
*Shortcuts – Personal Values – Harm
and Good Faith – Telling the Truth*

We have repeatedly looked at decision makers, estimated the effect alternative courses of action can have on all parties concerned, and stressed the need for a new discipline in our daily actions. The system of identifying the persons affected by a proposed decision, the fiduciary relationships, and ethical priorities is easier to apply in fiction than in daily life, where there isn't time for an extensive review. Shortcuts are needed.

Shortcuts

The pragmatic approach of greatest good/greatest number teaches that an action taken to achieve a personal goal at the expense of broader constituencies is "unethical." It is so easy to flatter ourselves in such circumstances and believe we have balanced the interests professionally. The ethical shortcut we have identified spells out our personal interest as a matter of routine.

In *The Ethics of Organizational Politics,* the authors address three shortcuts:

First, a decision maker can adopt some ideological system that reduces elaborate calculations of interest to a series of utilitarian rules. For example, some religious ideologies specify rules of behavior that, if followed, are supposed to result in an improved human condition (e.g., the "golden rule"). Certain organizational ideologies, such as professionalism, allow complex utilitarian calculations to be reduced to a focus on critical constituencies.

Second, a decision maker can adopt a simplified frame of reference in evaluating the interests of affected parties. For example, an economic frame of reference presupposes that alternatives are best evaluated in terms of dollar costs and dollar benefits. In this way, utilitarian calculations can be quantified.

And third, a decision maker can place boundaries on utilitarian calculations. For example, a decision maker can consider only the interests of those directly affected by a decision and thus exclude from analysis all indirect or secondary effects. Similarly, a decision maker can assume that by giving allegiance to a particular organizational coalition or set of goals (e.g., "official goals"), everyone's utilities will be optimized.[XV-1]

Some of these shortcuts have appeared in other chapters. We are also already familiar with ethical shortcuts from our own common use. They offer ways for each of us to get through a routine day a little more effectively. If you place both personal life goals and the values and goals of your firm on paper, you can use such shortcuts in an ordinary situation with some likelihood of achieving fairness. Being ethical requires us to be honest with ourselves about our limited wisdom, our inability to act in a fully unbiased and disinterested way, the limited amount of time we can reasonably spend analyzing and weighing alternatives in a typical day-to-day situation. In fact, shortcuts may be the only way for us to apply our skills in an ethical manner on a daily basis.

Every manager must put together a code of business conduct, at least on a subconscious level. It is more likely that one will adhere to the code if it is verbalized, and there is even more likelihood of adherence if all decision makers in a firm subscribe to the same general code. The real life code adopted by Northern Telecom offers a useful checklist for anyone drafting a personal business code or one for a company. Some of its major points are outlined below.[XV-2]

Fundamental Corporate Principles

- Profit is essential.
- Integrity is mandatory in all relationships.
- A corporation is accountable to its publics.

Operating Guidelines

- Keep employees informed of the issues affecting them.
- The corporation believes it is important to avoid or minimize commitments that might restrict the flexibility of its operations.
- The corporation does not reimburse any employee for personal political contributions.

Ethical Practice in the Marketplace

- Northern Telecom expects employees to be honest—with their employer, with its customers and other outside contacts, with their fellow workers, and with themselves.
- Customers deserve the highest quality product at reasonable prices.
- An ethical relationship with customers not only means the provision and service of superior products at reasonable prices, but also high business standards in all negotiations.
- Compensation of agents and representatives is commensurate with activities undertaken.

Northern Telecom is Part of Many Communities

- The local community.
- The international scientific community.
- Trade and professional organizations.
- The environment.

Ways to Contribute to a Community's Standard of Living

- Cooperate with organizations and individuals who make an effort to enhance the standing of the community.
- Financially support worthwhile community programs in such areas as social welfare, health, education, sports, arts, culture, and recreation.
- Encourage employees to take interest in local public affairs, charitable organizations, and other community projects.
- Consider the long-term interests of the community when selecting sites for new facilities.
- Express the Corporation's point of view on local and national issues that have a bearing on its operations.

Another shortcut is to quantify the effects of decisions on different groups, sometimes in accounting terms, sometimes on a numeric rating scale. Terminating a retirement plan represents more than the loss of vested benefits for employees. There is also some present value aspect to the loss of expected benefits from future continued employment. For older workers this can have greater significance because of a probable lack of mobility. If a plant is closed down, it is possible to quantify the dollar effects on the community in terms of social welfare, health, education, sports, arts, culture, and recreation.

There may be a productive aspect in selecting a plant site that will have long-term environmental, psychological, or aesthetic values that don't lend themselves to quantifications. The potential loss of confidence between Stan Smith and Martin Holyoke as a result of Holyoke's manipulation or misrepresentation in Erewhon discussed in Chapter 13 is not, at least on first examination, quantifiable in the same way as the difference between $21 and $24 a share. Yet its significance to the deal includes the effect on the directors influenced by Smith. It is not impossible to attach some symbols of significance that make it possible to provide comparison, even if Price Waterhouse could never audit them. Consider what would happen if the story of a manipulation appeared on the front page of the local papers. To an executive this situation may appear to stretch probabilities. But Smith and Holyoke found that the truth comes out. The negative impact of such a decision could be assessed by examining damage done on the public relations level and the costs of defending lawsuits, as long as there is an extra reference added for nonnumeric damage to a company. The use of a quantifiable rating can help put the argument in the realm of "how much" rather than "whether." The value of constructing a beautiful building may be even more difficult to quantify, but why not add a personal evaluation of bonus dollars-and-cents or a special "gold star" to help put the decision in perspective?

The "golden rule shortcut," often spoken in dulcet tones with an aspect of nobility, is: do unto others as you would have them do unto you. It can produce results that are considerably more selfish than those gained by practicing the adages of "love one another as I have loved you," or "love mercy, do justice, and walk humbly with your God." Nonetheless, as a shortcut it produces some practical results, especially when decisions are seen to create precedents. The rule is so general that the decision maker tends to assume a paternalistic role, often preventing other persons who had a right to participate in the decision from doing so. This need not occur if one of the "do unto me" choices relates to the form of reaching a decision as well as to the substance of that decision. Although the rule is most commonly and readily applied to simple bilateral interchanges, it can also apply to complex transactions.

Personal Values

For us as adults, our childhood baggage of virtues has traps as well as value, even "love your neighbor" and "do a good deed every day." Some ideals justify manipulation of others. None is specific enough to provide much insight into the increasingly complex situations we are trained to process as adults, situations that are full of contradictory considerations, short deadlines, and elusive facts. We need to revisit our own maxims.

The Time Management lecturer Charles Hobbs says "an individual cannot effectively manage without personal congruity, and congruity is not possible without clearly defined values that are brought under control in personal thought and performance."[XV-3] This in turn leads to his principle that "as you form a congruity between what you believe to be right and how you perform, you will experience the highest form of self-actualization." To nail down consistent corporate and personal goals for ourselves requires some work. However, we must articulate and prioritize our personal values in terms that are specific enough to be carried out through our actions or ethical shortcuts don't work.

Hobbs provides, as a prompter, examples of what one person may value most: honesty, self-esteem, family, humility, intelligence, and leadership. So stated, the glibness of these qualities makes them inadequate for our situation. However, as he points out, greater specificity results by simply turning the nouns into action statements: be honest; have self-esteem; love my family; be humble; grow intellectually; and be a leader.

Each of us should look at ways to start our own list. For instance, take the international scouting program's oath as an example:

> On my honor I will do my best to do my duty to God and my Country and to obey the Scout law; to help other people at all times; to keep myself physically strong, mentally awake, and morally straight.

And the Scout's law: "A scout is trustworthy, loyal, helpful, friendly, courteous, kind, obedient, cheerful, thrifty, brave, clean and reverent;" the Scout's motto, "Be prepared;" and the scout's slogan, "Do a good turn daily." Some of these points are more active and specific than others, although there is some incongruity; some points are pious and vague, some are old-fashioned, and some are even dangerous. Some, however, might be included on your own list of unifying principles. In the process of creating your own list you might test other lists, such as Moses' *Decalogue*. However presumptuous this may seem, prioritize the principles according to your perceptions, experience, and current responsibilities. The goal is to list *YOUR* most important values, ideals, aspirations, and tolerance of failure. Put them in your wallet. Revisit and revise them. Unless you recognize your values, you'll be unable to do strategic planning for yourself or your company, become an integrated person, or set long- and short-range goals that can carry you where you want to be. Beginning with a first draft of such principles you can massage, refine, and add to the list. Enrich the how, what, when, where, and why as you apply your principles to the discrete facts and situations encountered daily. The interplay of principles and actions illuminates both principles and actions; if they are not treated as clay to be molded situationally, the principles, unfortunately, may do more harm than good.

The Road to Oz

The validity of shortcuts depends on the foundation we provide. To firm them up we need to build up our skills. It is likely that an intern's shortcuts will be riskier than those of the experienced surgeon. Continuing the development of personal values results from and controls your experience. Without a personal value-base we cannot deal with fundamental human rights. Certainly a list of such rights has steadily grown in detail from the root of "life, liberty, and the pursuit of happiness" as a result of successful advocacy by affected groups and (not necessarily the same) more sensitive perceptions of the human condition. Perhaps "rights," the advocate's word, is too strong, too preemptive. A word that evokes less of a counterthrust may be better, a word that conveys the idea as a hope, an aspiration. So nuanced, the concept can be a more helpful tool of analysis than the peremptory phrase "my rights." In this country we begin with Bill of Rights categories: assembly, free speech, entitlement to equal protection under the laws, and proper notice; we then go on to disputed frontiers where society's interests and individualism meet: the "rights" of privacy, death, life, freedom of conscience, equal or subsidized employment, and free education.

The ethical theory of rights alerts us to the rights of others when we make a decision. The initial complication is that when we are affected by someone else's decision we are clear about our own rights, but considerably less conscious of the rights of others who are affected by our decisions. It seems clear that Holyoke did not think of the rights of Stan Smith as a professional when he instructed him to get his board of directors to ratify Holyoke's plan. Nor was it clear whose rights were being infringed upon by the rather careless whitewash job done by Mel Dean as investment banker to document a justification of the $21 a share price. Certainly the shareholders were being treated unjustly. The investment banking group was also professionally cheated by being manipulated into the position of the whitewash when asked to ratify the $21 stock price. The investment banker was cheating his own firm, too, by putting the firm's reputation behind an unprofessional piece of work.

Harm and Good Faith

Only in Utopia/Erewhon are ideal goals achieved. We have all been surprised when recommendations we have made, once accepted, have led to an unhappy and unanticipated result when our good faith "ought" to have produced a happy ending. This type of experience can make us gun-shy, leading us to avoid making future recommendations or causing us to become cynical. More constructively, it can help us to a maturity in searching for an ideology that reconciles the "ideal" and the "real" world. Every physician has had to come to grips with this issue. The physician's motto, "*primum non nocere*" (the first duty is to avoid causing harm), is the result. The motto, too, fails because it is hardly achievable: inaction can cause suffering, action can cause suffering. It is an undeniable fact that almost any decision can cause confusion and harm.

How can we take this fact into account when, like the surgeon, our explicit objective is not to *cause* harm? We can be legalistic and redefine the physician's motto for our "real world" situation, rephrasing it as "seek to minimize harm." In the end, however, we will harm others by failing to get all of the facts and their consequences completely straight.[XV-4]

We cannot be callous about causing harm, nor can we ignore the likelihood that at some point in our role as managers we will cause harm. When ethicists talk about the tragedy of the Ford Pinto automobile they tend to treat it as a paradigm of management indifference to prospective customer deaths, although there is a logical inconsistency in assuming that a consumer-oriented business will deliberately risk unnecessary deaths of the consumers and their passengers in order to sell cars.

We do not need to know the facts in order to see that life-threatening decisions should be sensitive, analytical, and based on values we can accept. Let's assume that a manager sought to identify the consequences of marketing a car known to have a potentially dangerous flaw, felt morally responsible for the consequences and weighed short-term profits against the risks of harm posed by the automobile. Could the manager be deemed ethical in proceeding with the production of the car if a redesign of its rear end costing 20 percent of the value of the car could limit the exposure of the gas tank during collisions and possibly reduce the chance of fatal accidents? 10 percent? 30 percent? We must remember that deaths are caused all the time by the use or abuse of cars.

To answer this, we have to go beyond simplistically equating "Pinto" and "management indifference." Something causes a decision to be made. Other factors to be considered in making the decision include the benefit of producing a successful small car in America, the number of jobs that could be created by producing the car, the possibility of reaping short-term profits from being the first American manufacturer to produce a small car, and plans to improve the design of future models. Yet, if there is always harm in the offing, how can we make an ethical decision? The automobile is not a drug that, in a time-bomb fashion, may be fatal to the purchaser without the intervention of an independent actor. Neither is it a chain saw that a maniac uses against his enemies, an action the manufacturer would be hard put to prevent. Is it the same as making a car with a very powerful engine, which the driver may misuse, causing his or others' deaths? Responding ethically, the issue of risk to its own passengers is dealt with if the car includes a roll bar, a padded dash and an air bag option—safety features designed to limit the risk of driving.

The hidden flaw in the original Ford Pinto, the vulnerable gas tank, is more subtle than these flaws or risks. The purchaser who drives carefully can be killed or injured by a statistically predictable event, the rear end expressway collision. Who will inform the consumer that purchasing a car will infringe on his or her rights? Insurance companies can refuse to insure cars that are damage-prone unless the owners pay substantial premiums; they may also be able to deny insurance payments to claimants who do not abide by the seat belt law. When you reach people's pocketbooks you force their attention to the risk. Would not an educational campaign by the insurance industry represent a desirable combination of self-interest and pastoral responsibility? Should fast-and-light cars be prohibited?

Is education enough? Is the Surgeon General's warning about cigarettes an effective approach to notifying the public about the dangers of cigarettes? The government has its own conflicts in this situation: maintaining jobs for the tobacco industry's workers; concern about smuggling; the health of smokers and their neighbors; votes from nonsmokers; votes from smokers; the benefit of tax revenues to the federal government. Does the self-interest of the government as tax collector and political machine cloud the propriety of the information decision? Should cigarette use be prohibited by the federal government, or is the violation of individual rights justified? Is disclosure of risks the better rule?

Such questions do not yield prompt answers even if we are advocates and know the specifics and the context of a situation; however, they need to be asked if we are to learn to use rights as an ethical tool. The rights of those affected by a product are rather clearly infringed upon if there is an increased likelihood of death as a result of using the product. But automobiles and lung cancer are not the only steel balls whirling about at the end of the nearby crane. If dairy products and beef increase the chance of arterio-sclerosis and coronary heart disease, should the television networks carry their ads? If shareholders vote for a poison pill that is being given to them by their management should Congress overrule share-holder power? The right of the members of our society to make free choices can be a "higher" ethic than the right to be protected.

That we have a right to be protected from government interventions does not relieve us of the personal ethical job of not causing harm by our actions. It is not enough to make a commitment that we will avoid harming people. Not harming people is an ideal, a goal, and ideals are helpful; harming people is a norm not an exception, whether by a dangerous drug or a sharp tongue. In each situation each of us must draw a line based on our experience, our responsibility in making the decision, and the viable alternative. Despite our best intentions we will indeed cause harm, and we need to accept this reality in order to limit the harm we will cause. We need to say:

> In my professional sphere I have a moral responsibility. Life is action and I will act. The fact that harm may occur is something I will not ignore. I will not pretend it can not occur or that the incidental harm is necessarily for the best. The harm may come from the very act of my intervention. I will not be able to avoid harm. But I will seek to limit the damage I cause by my action and inaction, realizing the consequences as fully as possible. That is the only way I can respect the rights of those affected.

Telling the Truth

Perceptions of justice, equity, fairness, and impartiality are short-cuts. As viewed by Cavanagh/Moberg/Velasquez,[XV-5] there must also be a built-in compensatory response by the corporation when injuries are caused by the corporation. This helps us see an ethical remedy to MassCon's failure to act fairly in its disclosure to the NHSI shareholders discussed in Chapter 13. It is all very well to say that the $21 price caused the shareholders to profit, but the fact remains that their "trustees," the directors of NHSI, were misled. *Caveat emptor* is not an ethical doctrine that supersedes the right to truth. Will the rights of some other group be less likely to be infringed upon in the future if this corporation, MassCon, must compensate NHSI shareholders for cheating them? If so, how should that be done? The meeting can be undone and MassCon directed to begin again with a fair disclosure. But if MassCon instead decides to retain its holding of stock, rescinding the $21 a share offer and leaving the minority in with $14 shares, the "solution" is no solution.

Trying to combine the ideologies of pragmatism, rights, and justice can be confusing. It adds an extra dimension to a result, but is it really necessary? Does the extra time and tension improve the result? When one coherent logical system meshes with another coherent logical system a new system of logic and consistency does not necessarily result. However, we are groping for straws: for guidelines, perceptions, and tools.

Ultimately, it is the manager on the spot who will make the management decision, and that person's integrity will have a great deal to do with the result. In one case a clearly unjustifiable impact of harm to one constituency will dominate the decision; in another case it will be necessary to search out the voiceless, recognizing their unexpressed needs as rights that merit special consideration. In a third case it may be unproductive to establish a hierarchy of rights, and the answer may be to act impartially in relation to persons within the same group and get on with the job.

Looking back at the MassCon/NHSI merger process, we can see the need to establish some rules on when to tell the truth. Failure to do that undermines an entire set of relationships. Yet, we have many explanations and excuses for not telling the truth. Our society makes it easy not to tell the truth. From the doctor with the cancer patient to the parent with the young child, we are brought up on the usefulness of the "devil's truth," the "white lie." Our system for the distribution of goods, services, and ideas is built on hyperbole, and a generation of Americans has replaced precise nouns with the universal word "thing." It is not easy to find the truth or to tell it. Telling the truth is not enough unless we present it in such a way that the truth is heard by the person to whom it is directed: the communication must be market-oriented and fashioned in accordance with the sophistication and experience of the listener. The substantive core of a sophisticated idea can be communicated to a child and be true; in the same form it would be a fairy story to a college freshman. The flaw lies not in the college freshman but in the communication.

Two primary areas of lying occurred in the MassCon/NHSI situation: the statements Holyoke made to Stan Smith to get him going with his board, and the whitewash by the investment banking team. At best Holyoke gave the substantive core to a person who needed details. It would appear that he saw the MassCon shareholders as his only constituency. He is spending their money, he works for them, and he has come up with a price for the shares of NHSI:

not the theoretical price of the feasibility committee, but a price that is defensible and will work in the market without squandering corporate money. Twenty-four dollars was a maximum and something over the $14 market was a minimum. He might have "split" it at $19. But $21 had some history. It was his job to make a deal and in his view the board of NHSI represented him. He did his job. What he missed was the series of events set in motion by lying.

As to the investment banking group, the problem is not that they shortcut the investigation. They had limited time and produced the necessary papers. They had a job to do and, with one not-so-minor exception, they did it. The problem was that they produced a document supporting an undesignated appraisal price that was to be provided to those without investment banking skills in a way designed to cause them (the public) to rely on the bankers' professionalism. But their boss on the board was not the appraiser; it was Holyoke.

We see *paternalism* by Holyoke in making and executing the unilateral decision. We see his *coercion* of Stan Smith, and in turn other people, and the investment banker's *coercion* of his people. There is a violation of the *rights* and *personal integrity* of those who have been coerced or misled. The possibility of effective *participation* by the NHSI shareholders was eliminated, although they did vote on the question and appeared to *participate*. There was also a group failure to deal *justly* and fairly with the minority shareholder, and an ignorance of the *conflicts of interest* in the transaction. This was an example of a *utilitarian* process dominated by self-interest and a poor precedent for the future.

If there is a single remedial step that hindsight suggests on the NHSI/MassCon merger, it is to provide staff support for the independent directors. Even if such support were not available on a general basis, it could be instituted for complex policy and conflict decisions. MassCon may not have been acting in bad faith. A lot of the mistakes could have reflected the haste that seemed to be imposed by deadlines for the filing of proxy materials, the difficulty of postponing a meeting, and a *déjà vu* attitude toward the transaction. If this is so, management might have reacted favorably to any director who urged the hiring of an independent counselor, legal or financial, as an extra pair of eyes to see past the haste in which the decision had to be made. Someone was needed who could educate the directors and, in turn, the shareholders on the ethical and policy implications of the corporate actions.

To the extent management is a profession, it needs clearly stated standards of practice addressing ethics and loyalties. The profession does not have an "either/or" loyalty, it has many loyalties. Its decisions ultimately are "go or no go," but they are based on as much information as possible. Business builds its products on market estimates. It commits its funds in light of unverifiable macro projections. It knows how to deal with intangibles; it has the training and skill to deal with the rights and expectations of groups that may conflict with one another, and assumes responsibility when in the end one group always fares less well than the other.

Similarly, security analysts and portfolio managers need more training and information on how they can (and should and are expected to) represent shareholders. They, too, need personal pre-published standards.

If virtue is not its own reward, consider this: together directors and analysts have a joint opportunity to replace specific legislative and judicial regulation that they dislike with private-sector responsibility for balancing unbridled self-interest. From the rash of legislative responses to the "takeover game" it should be recognized that failure to establish structures that deal with conflicting interests in a fair way invites substantially expanded government response. The opportunity to develop our own more appropriate response to ethical dilemmas will be replaced by the thoughtless following of someone else's structure and form.

The Road from Oz

Where do we go from here? *Finnegan's Wake* [XV-6] ends with the beginning fragment of a sentence: "A way a lone a last a loved a long the." The sentence continues as the first words of the book: "riverrun past Eve and Adam's, from swerve of shore to bend of bay, bring us by a commodius vicus of recirculation back to Howth Castle and Environs." At best, the ending of this book is a beginning, allowing each of us to begin scratching out the personal blueprint of our future actions all over again.

Footnotes

I-1   Concern with the effect of actions is sometimes referred to as "act/utilitarian ethics;" concern with the way actions may influence later actions by way of precedent is sometimes referred to a "rule/utilitarian ethics." As choice of theory can prompt different decisions, both theories must be applied. cf. Harold F. Williams "Do Regulations Reinforce Ethical Postures?" a speech given at Hebrew Union College, November 13, 1980.

I-2   Over fifty years ago Adolph A. Berle, Jr. and Gardiner C. Means (*The Modern Corporation and Private Property;* New York: Macmillan, 1932) focused attention on the *de facto* shift to management from shareholders of corporate control and its social implications. See also Merrick Dodd "For Whom are Corporate Managers Trustees?" *Harvard Business Review* 45 (1932). Benjamin Graham and David L. Dodd, *Security Analysis,* (New York: McGraw-Hill, 1934).

I-3   By 1970, concerns for issues of corporate social responsibility were being demonstrated on college campuses. Charles W. Powers, Jon P. Gunnerman, and John G. Simon responded with a gem of a book: *The Ethical Investor - Universities and Corporate Responsibility* (New Haven: Yale University Press, 1972). See also: Ellen Berek, Ed. *Williams as a Responsible Investor,* (April 1983, Williams College) and Walter Williams "Beware the Well Intentioned," *The New York Times,* May 15, 1983.

I-4   A majority of the boards of directors of mutual funds managed by Scudder, Stevens & Clark consists of unaffiliated directors. Nominating committees for independent directors consist solely of independents.

I-5   Frank H. Esterbrook and Daniel R. Fishel, "The Proper Role of a Target's Management in Responding to a Tender Offer," *Harvard Law Review,* April, 1981. Cf. Peter F. Drucker "Ethical Chic," *Forbes,* September 14, 1981.

I-6   In his article "Corporate Takeovers and Professional Investors" (*Financial Analysts Journal,* January/February 1983, pp. 75-80), Walter S. Morris defined the professionalism of security analysts as including a dimension of ethical imagination. Mr. Morris' invitation to the dance has been implemented by The Institute of Chartered Financial Analysts and The Financial Analysts Federation in their *Standards of Practice Handbook,* (see third edition, 1986). See also: James F.

Bresnahan S.J., "Ethics and the Study and Practice of Law: The Problem of Being Professional in a Fuller Sense," *Journal of Legal Education,* Vol. 28, No. 2 (1976) and "Ethical Theory and Professional Responsibility: Possible Contributions of Religious Ethics to Dialogue about Professional Ethics of Attorneys," *The Jurist* (1976); Harold B. Williams, "The Role of Law in Society," a speech given to the Legal Aid Society of New York, April 23, 1976; Peter F. Drucker, "What is 'Business Ethics'," *The Public Interest,* Spring 1981.

II-1   "Excess parachute payment" was defined in the Tax Reform Act of 1984, Internal Revenue Code 280G. Corporations may not deduct from income a compensation payment that is contingent on a change in ownership or control and amounts to three or more times the employee's base salary.

II-2   Professor Barton Leach was a vintage star at Harvard Law School, specializing in property interests. The superiority of perception of a decisionmaker on the spot is noted in Leach, *Cases and Materials on Future Interests 240* (2nd Edition 1940).

IV-1   One of the most vicious forms of acquisition can be loans to the raider financed by assets of the target. The bank does not pay over cash until the tender is successfully in hand.

V-1   The intuition of a knowledge worker, at its best, embodies reasoning and foresight. Yet, as even knowledge workers' personalities are flawed, conscious analysis is required: if an expert's intuition is to reject a scheme supported by analysis, more homework is needed. If the homework does not turn up enough supporting specifics, the hunch may be misplaced. A vague global concern about the justice of an issue deserves attention but is rarely enough by itself. An expert's intuition in such a case may be sentimentalized by loose thinking, just as an amateur's intuition about the solution to a complex situation often can be more misleading than constructive. This is especially so if the result advances self-interest.

VI-1   Reverend Leon Sullivan has served for many years as a member of the General Motors Board of Directors. His proposal for specific corrective measures for South African operations began with modest goals to encourage self-esteem and economic progress such as those developed for improvement in the Southeastern United States in 1948: desegregate toilet facilities, bus terminals, and department stores; equal pay for equal work. The Sullivan Principles, as they are called, also cover training for increased job responsibility. Reverend Sullivan is now grappling with this ethical hurdle: there is a real benefit to specific South African workers of Sullivan-principled U.S. companies in South Africa, yet there is harm to blacks generally by helping to stabilize a society that denies the equality of blacks as human beings. Cf. "Participation III - Atlantic Richfield and Society" (Atlantic Richfield Company).

VI-2   "The boarhound and the boar/Pursue their pattern as before/But reconciled among the stars," "Burnt Norton" T.S. Eliot, *Four Quartets* (Harcourt Brace & Co., New York, 1943).
That does not imply that there is no meaning to the ritual of two antagonists, but rather that the meaning can exist *because* of the two; so long as each is true to its own vision. See also: Herman Kahn, "Bishops & The Bomb," *The New York Times,* December, 1982; Gary Zukav, *The Dancing Wu Li Masters, An Overview of the New Physics* (New York: William Morrow, 1979).

VI-3   Resolutions mandating directors to establish ethical guidelines for their companies have been proposed to Rockwell International, Emerson Electric, GTE, General Electric, McDonnell Douglas, and Raytheon. See also: R.M. Hare, "Rules of War and Moral Reasoning," *War and Moral Responsibility*, (Princeton University Press, 1974).

VI-4 The Investor Responsibility Research Center (1319 F Street, NW, Suite 900, Washington, D.C. 20004) has published these booklets in the area of military contracts: *The Nuclear Weapons Industry* (1984) and *Stocking the Arsenal: A Guide to the Nation's Top Military Contractors* (1985).

VI-5 See *The Investment Manager's Handbook*, ed. Sumner N. Levine, Dow Jones - Irwin, (Homewood, Illinois, 1980). In Chapter 24: "Legal Limits on Investing," I expressed my concern about noninvestment-related proxy votes and portfolio selection. Whose political views control? Can a manager properly pursue a personal "hobby horse," however noble, without regard to the views of the investors? Priorities, costs, and results must be objectively addressed as well as the need to identify and resolve inconsistent client instructions. (See page 681 ff..) That issue is argued often in terms of the duty of elected officials: is it to use their heads and judgments or to mirror their constituents' views? See also *Conflicts of Interest in the Proxy Voting Systems,* James E. Heard and Howard D. Sherman (Investor Responsibility Research Center, Inc., Washington, D.C., 1987); Tamar Frankel, "Decision Making for Social Investing" (Chapter 8) *Social Investing,* (Dan M. McGill, ed.), Pension Research Council: Richard D. Irwin, Illinois 1984.

VI-6 T.S. Eliot writes "love of a country/Begins as attachment to our own field of action/And comes to find that action of little importance/Though never indifferent." "Little Gidding," *Four Quartets, supra.*

VI-7 A challenge: what kind of analysis can you make of the military contracts resolution? Consider yourself to be a security analyst making a recommendation to an individual client with respect to the vote. First, treat the shareholder proposal as a series of resolutions, each of which deals with one of the proposed areas for the development of ethical criteria by the board. Then put yourself in the shoes of a director of Canfield with this proposal. How would you vote and clarify your vote on the overall proposal? Systematic analysis and the casting of the vote are synergistic and separate.

Look at the persons affected to see what groups are relying upon you and your judgment. As a director you are a representative in whom the present shareholders have placed trust, but you also represent employees, management, and future owners of Canfield. You even have some obligation to do justice to the communities in which your employees live and Canfield does business. There are suppliers (and their employees) and customers (and their employees) who also depend on the fairness of your decision. You are also a member of the world community of human beings.

Is there a proper distinction between your taking action that, intervening, causes harm and your not taking action when certain foreseeable harmful results could have been forestalled by action?

VII-1 *Palsgraf vs. Long Island Railroad Co.,* New York Court of Appeals, 1928, 248 NY 339.

VII-2 *Kinsman Transit Co.,* U.S. Court of Appeals, 2d Cir., 1964, 338 F.2d 708.

VII-3 Stanley Hauerwas, *Truthfulness and Tragedy - Further Investigations into Christian Ethics* (University of Notre Dame Press, Indiana, 1977), especially

Chapter 5 with David B. Burrell: "Self Deception and Autobiography: Reflections on Speer's *Inside the Third Reich.*"

VIII-1   Henry B. Arthur, "Making Ethics Work," *Strategic Management Journal* Vol. 5, 319-325.

VIII-2   What if Grinnell, upon further questioning, reported that an extra layer of armor was added by agreement of the DOS/X board to indemnify SSI against any liability in connection with the option, further inhibiting a potential buyer from going to court to block the option as manipulative?

VIII-3   "Agnes White's Corollary," from a *New Yorker* magazine article of thirty years ago, dealt with a rule so universal that it applied to taxes, marriage, and owning a dog: "everything is easier to get into than to get out of." (cf. *Data Probe Corp. v. Datatab, Inc.,* 568 F. Supp. 1538 (S.D.N.Y.) rev'd 722 F. 2d I (2d Cir. 1983.) See also: John G. Gillis and John L. Casey, "Ethical Considerations," *Takeovers and Shareholders: The Mounting Controversy,* DeMong and Peavey, eds. (Financial Analysts Research Foundation, Charlottesville, Virginia, 1985, pp. 51-59).

IX-1   In the mid 1970s Congress took a number of investor protection steps, placing limits on the discretionary management of investments by firms also acting as brokers, (Section 11a, Securities Exchange Act of 1934 as amended.) Cf. "The Accountable Regulator," Harold Williams, a speech given at the 1981 "S.E.C. Speaks" Conference.

IX-2   Batterymarch Financial Management of Boston has programmed its computers to select both the security and the executing broker, based on Batterymarch inputs of desired portfolio shape and security characteristics with inputs from brokers as to availability and prices of securities, and commission levels (the computers are named Fred and Allyn).

IX-3   Ethical management demands follow-through when authority is delegated to anyone, even the President. Securities Exchange Act of 1934 Release #23640; Investment Advisers Act of 1940 Release #1038. The "smoking gun," there, was an account where transactions could be back dated: certain purchases for the client, which went up in market value between trade and settlement dates, were transferred to others; purchases that decreased in value in that five-day period were left for the pension fund. See Peter Berger, "On the Obsolescence of the Concept of Honor," *The Homeless Mind: Modernization and Consciousness* (New York: Random House, 1973).

X-1   As the constitutions of the exchanges expressly prohibited customer rebates of all or part of the commissions, the average advisor had little knowledge about how to "recapture" commissions without violating the "anti-rebate" rules. What could be done practically was also unclear.

The invitation to "Buy Your Office Furniture Through Us With Commission Dollars on Client Accounts" was an invitation that was easy to turn down on ethical grounds. The concept that there was a legal obligation as a fiduciary to test the validity of anti-rebate rules in order to recapture for the benefit of *your client* 40 percent of commissions paid to executing brokers was ethically and legally confusing, as well as operationally complex.

X-2   Many critics identify low commission rates as a cause of high portfolio turnover. Some say that third-party consultant pressures on pension funds to seek short-term performance have been the reason for the high volume, others say that the pressure on commissions is largely stimulated by new entrants into the brokerage business who provide minimal services beyond execution.

X-3   Julie Rohrer, "Soft Dollar Boom in Third Party Research," *Institutional Investor,* April 1974.

XI-1   Jeremy Rifkin and Randy Barber, *The North Will Rise Again-Pension, Politics, and Power in the 1980s* (Beacon Press, Boston, 1978). The authors seek to alert trade union managers about tools for job protection: invest pension assets in companies with a strong trade union bias, reject investments in nonunion companies, buy securities of companies in depressed areas, encourage companies that use underutilized unionized skills. Reject investments in companies that trade in South Africa, at a minimum to support black union members and the coherence of the labor movement. See Roy A. Schotland, "But the Pension was Just Sitting There," 1981, *Pension World*; Laurence Litvak, *Pension Funds & Economic Renewal,* (1981 Council of State Planning Agencies, 400 North Capital Street, Washington, D.C. 20001).

XI-2   A very useful record on the subject was made before the ERISA Advisory Council of the U.S. Department of Labor at the June 14, 1983, National Pension Forum on Social Investment.

XII-1   Texas Gulf Sulfur and Morgan Guaranty Trust, among other companies, have grappled with this aspect of sensational news.

XII-2   The word "exploitation" has only a pejorative connotation today, presumably because of our awareness of improprieties and excesses. The word "discrimination" has suffered a similar "sea change."

XII-3   A dramatic use of this process of larger ethical identification concerns the approach to nuclear weapons by religious groups weighing the peril of mass extinction against freedom of the individual.

XIII-1   Cf. *Weinberger v. UOP, Inc.,* 457 A2d 701 (Delaware Supreme Court 1983); Richard T. de George, *Business Ethics* (Macmillan, New York 1986). "There is such a thing as loyalty upward. If I do you'll get loyalty downward. If I don't—well, I'll find out why, and I'll see to it that I do."—Captain Queeg (Herman Wouk, *The Caine Mutiny*; New York: Doubleday, 1951).

XIV-1   The recapture by the sponsor of the surplus of a terminated pension fund is subject to a review by the Internal Revenue Service: the corporation must bring back into taxable income amounts that had previously been deducted and are now being returned to the corporation. The Department of Labor is also interested, reflecting its concern that the beneficiaries receive the benefits to which they were entitled. To encourage corporations to achieve full funding of benefits, there has been a tax incentive (deductibility), a sanction (for lack of full funding), and a safety net (authority for the sponsor to recapture excess assets on plan termination).

XIV-2   Robert Bolt, *A Man for All Seasons* (New York: Vintage Books—Random House, 1960); also, Stanley Hauerwas and Thomas L. Schaffer, "Hope Faces Power: Thomas More and the King of England," *Soundings,* pp. 456-479 (Winter 1975).

XV-1   In "The Ethics of Organizational Politics," *Academy of Management Review* 6, July 1981 pp. 363-374, the authors (Cavanagh, Moberg and Velasquez) propose several shortcuts, not to free the decisionmaker from moral responsibility, but to increase the probability of desirable, though "suboptimum," outcomes.

XV-2   English language copies of its excellent fifteen-page *Code of Business Conduct* are available through Corporate Relations Department/Northern Telecom Limited/P.O. Box 458, Station A/ Missisauga, Ontario, Canada L5A 3A2.

XV-3   Charles R. Hobbs, *The Insight System for Planning your Time and your Life,*: a two day seminar, audio cassettes of which are distributed by Nightingale-Conant, Chicago.

XV-4   The morality of dislocation and harm caused by those with the best intentions in the world is illuminated by Stanley Hauerwas in *Truthfulness and Tragedy, supra;* Charles W. Powers and David Vogel, *Ethics in the Education of Business Managers,* (1980, The Hastings Center).

XV-5   *The Ethics of Organizational Politics, supra.*

XV-6   James Joyce, *Finnegans Wake* (New York: The Viking Press, 1944).